SCIENTIFIC EVIDENCE

FOR THE

SECOND COMING OF CHRIST

SCIENTIFIC EVIDENCE

FOR THE

SECOND COMING OF CHRIST

by John Zachary

Harvard House
Denver, Colorado

Copyright © 1993 by John Zachary. All Rights Reserved. No part of this work may be reproduced or transmitted in any form or by any means, electronic or mechanical, including photocopying and recording, or by any information storage or retrieval system, except as may be expressly permitted by the 1976 Copyright Act or in writing by the Publisher. Requests for permission should be addressed to Permissions, Harvard House, P.O. Box 24221, Denver, Colorado 80224.

Printed in the U.S.A.

All Scripture quotations in this publication are from the Holy Bible, New International Version. Copyright © 1973, 1978, 1984 International Bible Society. Used by permission of Zondervan Bible publishers.

ISBN: 0-9640404-0-9 Science & Religion Series
ISBN: 0-9640404-3-3 (Volume 2)

ILLUSTRATION CREDIT

We are grateful for permission to reproduce drawings by Jennifer in Chapter 4.

ABOUT THE AUTHOR

John Zachary graduated with honors in Mathematics (SNU) and History (CSU). He is employed as a reliability engineer. Twenty years of research have been devoted to the preparation and theory of this book.

Contents

Chapter   **Page**

	Introduction	1
1	Bridging Science to Faith	3
2	Separating Science from Faith	13
3	Unraveling Prophecy with Astronomy	15
4	Prophetic Blueprints	21
5	The First Coming: A Lunar Appraisal	31
6	Christ's Return: The Lunar Junction	45
7	The Unknown Factor	49

Appendices

A	The Reign of Artaxerxes	53
B	Day of Preparation	59
C	Lunar Dating the Crucifixion	61
D	Other Views of Daniel's Prophecy	67

Charts

A	Hebrew Calendar	71
B	Egyptian Calendar	72

References	73
Preparations	76

Dedication

To Kay, whose devotion has tremendously improved *Scientific Evidence for the Second Coming of Christ*.

Introduction

The earth we live on is a science laboratory. The moon consistently circles the earth. In turn, the earth and moon circle the sun. Day by day, the heavens consistently travel their natural path, providing information to evaluate our past and future.

Scientific Evidence for the Second Coming of Christ illuminates "time-oriented" Scripture with ancient lunar eclipses and lunar cycles, archeological discoveries centuries before Christ lived, and secular (nonreligious) writings. My inquiry reveals what appears to be the design of man's history: a divine plan that unfolds in the 5th century BC and ends in the 21st century.

Many will believe the results of my research outright. Others will question the validity of the inquiry. I must emphasize that this book is theoretical. However, I will not be surprised to witness the future fulfillment of conclusions presented in *Scientific Evidence for the Second Coming of Christ.*

I pray that you will join me in discovering the ancient mystery described in this book. We stand on the brink of a great revelation, clearly revealed in the heavens by the Ancient of Days.

Scientific Evidence for the Second Coming of Christ supplements Chapters 3 and 5, and Appendices A, C, D & F in my first book, ***Threshold of Eternity.***

Chapter 1

Bridging Science to Faith

Mouths gaped wide open as the red-nosed puppet seemed to slip, then catch himself.

"Wow!" echoed across the audience.

Enchanted by the show, I chuckled as I began to identify with the lively puppet. Suddenly, my arms and legs moved up and down as if strings pulled from above. "Oh Stop!" I screamed.

Dozens of eyes turned to stare at me. "Stop what, man?"

"Nothing," I said, as my head motioned left to right under the sway of a domineering force.

Earthly Puppets

Are events on earth directed from heaven? Could there be a theatrical show by which people act a part, just like a puppet? I have discovered a divine plan written in the heavens that shows you and I are being directed.

How can we know that a Supreme Being is directing you and me?

The only way to uncover supernatural direction in human events is to consider the prophetic utterances of ancient men. For example, Daniel, who lived about 2,600 year ago, foretold of Jerusalem's future. When we use astronomy to pinpoint exact dates of predicted events for Jerusalem, then we will detect a plan by which humanity is being directed.

For example, Daniel predicted Jerusalem's destruction by Rome in AD 70. Consider Daniel's words.

Scientific Evidence

The people of the ruler who will come will destroy the city [Jerusalem] *and the sanctuary* [temple] (Dan. 9:26).

Daniel specifies that the Jewish temple would be destroyed. Can we figure out the exact day of the temple's destruction using astronomy?

We can pinpoint the exact day the Jewish temple burned to the ground in AD 70, using astronomy as will be shown later. The result of finding out when predicted events occurred shows that man's history has been predetermined.

Consider the gravity of this question. If a Supreme Being controls man's history and astronomy can pinpoint when predicted events occurred, is it possible to foresee our future with the accuracy of mathematics?

Consider the magnitude of my answer and twenty years of research. **Scientific dating of biblical events shows we can clearly see our future.**

Astronomy's Link to Prophecy

When the earth's shadow crosses the moon, a lunar eclipse occurs. Astronomers can predict future lunar and solar eclipses through mathematics. Astronomers are akin to prophets in their ability to predict future events.

But an astronomer is not a prophet. The Spirit directed the prophets. Pious men listened to the Almighty and spoke His words.

Astronomers, unlike prophets, predict the future by the exact laws of physics. There is no spiritual leading for the astronomer.

Yet, there is a fundamental link between the prophet and the astronomer. We can sum up this link as follows: **Sometimes the prophets predicted events that happened at the time of a new moon, a full moon, or even New Year's Day.**

Bridging Science to Faith

In the Bible, faith is tied to astronomy as the heavens relate to events in Christ's life:

Do not let anyone judge you . . . with regard to a religious festival, **a New Moon celebration** *or a Sabbath Day. These are* **a shadow of the things that were to come**; *the reality, however, is found in Christ* (Col. 2:17-18)

This verse links the time of a new moon to the future or as, *"a shadow of the things that were to come."* We have a meager glimpse of how a new moon points to future biblical events.

To clarify how astronomy links to prophecy, I will use the example of how scientific dating pinpoints the day Rome set fire to the Jewish temple in AD 70. This example will begin to show the foundational theory of my research.

Destruction of the Temple in AD 70

Roman legions set fire to the temple and the eastern part of Jerusalem on Sunday, August 5, AD 70. The writings of Josephus, a secular Jewish historian who witnessed the destruction, support this date.

Josephus observed the temple's burning on the 10th day of the fifth Jewish month called Av. Josephus noted that Babylon burned the temple on the same date in prior history. Josephus' evidence reads:

Titus retired into the tower of Antonia, and resolved to storm the temple the next day, early in the morning, with his whole army, and to encamp round about the holy house; but, as for that house, God had for certain long ago doomed it to the fire; and now **that fatal day** was come, according to the revolution of ages; <u>**it was the tenth day of the month Lous [Av]**</u>, **upon which it was formerly burnt by the king of Babylon.**[1]

Josephus reveals that the Romans set fire to the temple on the 10th day of the fifth Jewish month. The Hebrew calen-

Scientific Evidence

dar is based on the moon. We must convert Josephus' lunar date to a solar date that we can understand, such as August 5th.[a] I will use charts to illustrate how Josephus' lunar date converts to a solar date.

The first day of any Hebrew month begins with a new moon. Since Josephus reveals the temple burned on the 10th day of the month, we know ten days had passed since a new moon. Since the fifth Hebrew month, Av, contains 30 days, 20 days remained to the next month as shown in this chart.

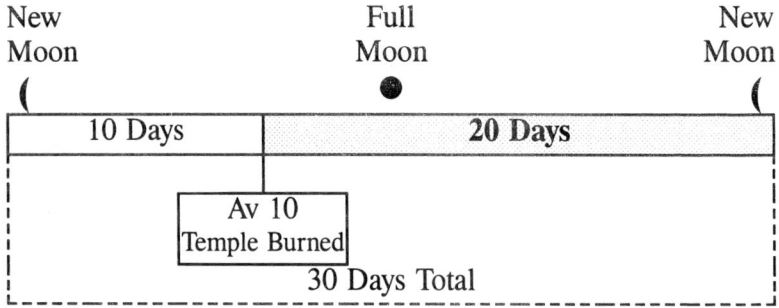

We visually understand by this chart that the temple burned 20 days before the next new moon.

The sixth Jewish month, called Elul, contains 29 days. Let's add the 20 days left in the fifth Jewish month, Av, to the 29 days in the sixth Jewish month, Elul. This totals 49 days as follows.

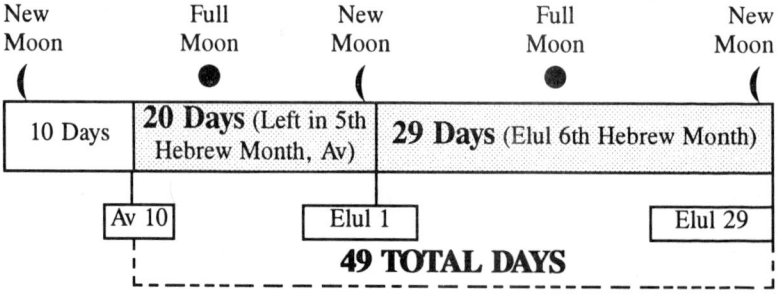

Bridging Science to Faith

We can understand visually how there were 49 days counted in this manner.

Finally, the Jewish New Year occurs on the first day of the seventh Hebrew month, called Tishri. We add one day to the 49 days to equal 50 total days. This means that the Romans set fire to the temple 50 days before the new moon in September, AD 70. Following is a chart showing this idea.

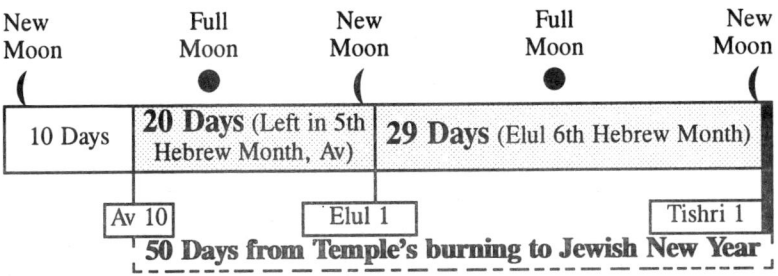

We grasp visually that the Romans burned the temple 50 days before the new moon in September, AD 70. We simply find the time of the new moon on an astronomical chart and subtract 50 days.[b]

The 50 day counting gives us one fact for pinpointing the day Rome set fire to the temple. Josephus gives us a second detail that reveals the temple's burning occurred on a Sunday. Josephus writes about what the Jewish people did the day before the temple burned.

On this day the Jews were so weary, and under such consternation, that they refrained from any attacks.[2]

Josephus implies that the day before the temple burned was a Sabbath, which is Saturday. This means the Romans set fire to the temple on a Sunday.

The 50 day counting and Sunday burning allow us to pinpoint the day on which the temple burned. When we count back 50 days from the new moon in September, AD 70, we must come to a Sunday.

Scientific Evidence

Astronomical charts show that a new moon occurred on Sunday, September 23, AD 70, at 5:21 a.m.[3] Ideal times for the first day of the lunar month could have been from Saturday, September 22 to Wednesday, September 26. However, when we count back 50 days to a Sunday, there is only one answer. The Jewish New Year occurred on Monday, September 24. Fifty days before September 24 brings us to Sunday, August 5, AD 70, as follows:

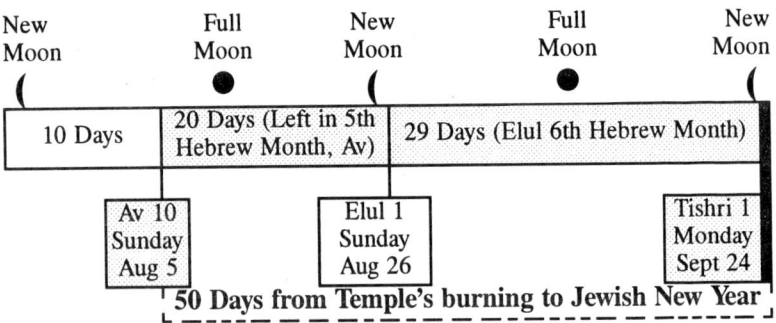

Astronomy and the secular writings of Josephus enable us to pinpoint the day Rome set fire to the temple. Astronomy naturally relates to Daniel's prophecy.

Show Me the Design of Man's History

Pinpointing when the temple burned down does NOT reveal the design of man's history. I must show when other predicted events occurred using astronomy and archaeology. After we pinpoint several of Daniel's predicted events, then we can measure the time between the events, which appears to show the design of man's history.

Let's consider two other events which Daniel predicted for Jerusalem. I will give you a general outline of Daniel's prophecy at this point.

Daniel's "time-oriented" prophecy began on March 14, 445 BC, with a decree to rebuild the charred ruins of Jerusalem. Daniel wrote of this decree:

***From the issuing of the decree to restore and rebuild Jerusalem** until the Anointed One* [Messiah], *the ruler, comes* (Dan. 9:25).

Next, Daniel prophesied the Messiah would appear at Jerusalem. Astronomical and biblical evidence show the Messiah entered Jerusalem on April 6, AD 32.

Daniel's third event occurred when Rome burned Jerusalem in AD 70. Succeeding chapters will show how astronomy pinpoints the dates cited above. I have outlined Daniel's predictions from left to right as follows:

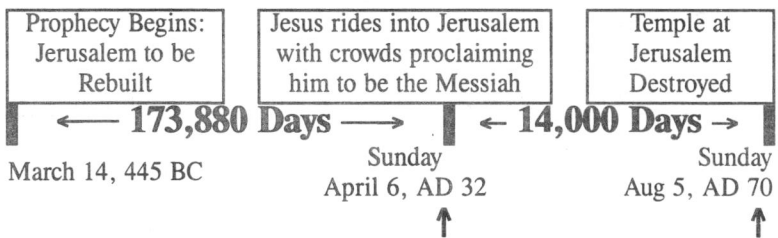

On the right side of this chart, 14,000 days stand out. Arrows point to the events that uncover the 14,000 days. We count the days from Jesus' entry into Jerusalem as the Messiah to the temple's burning.[c] The number 14,000, by itself, expresses design.

However, the 14,000 days occurred almost two thousand years ago. Is this prophecy relevant to the 20th century?

Oracle for the 21st Century

Daniel's predictions extend into the 21st century. We will find that judgment came upon the generation of Hebrews who rejected Jesus as their Messiah. The length of that generation was 14,000 days. Let's consider how the 14,000 days pertain to the 1st century, and then to the 21st century.

When Jesus entered Jerusalem as the Messiah, he confronted the corrupt leaders of Israel. Jesus prophesied to

Scientific Evidence

Israel's leaders of Jerusalem's future wrecking by Rome, warning that generation:

> *Upon you will come all the righteous blood that has been shed on earth,. . . . I tell you the truth, all this will come upon* **THIS GENERATION** (Matt. 23:35-36).

Daniel's 14,000 days measure the generation that rejected Jesus as their Messiah.

Prophecy for the 21st Century

Jesus, just like Daniel, predicted Rome's leveling of Jerusalem in AD 70. Yet, Jesus' prediction about Jerusalem reaches into the 20th century. The Messiah proclaimed.

> *Jerusalem will be trampled on by the Gentiles* [Beginning with the Romans on August 5, AD 70] *until the times of the Gentiles are fulfilled* [Ending with Jordan on June 7, 1967] (Luke 21:24b).

Gentile nations controlled Jerusalem for 1,897 years. So Jesus' prophecy for Jerusalem started with Rome in AD 70 and ended with Jordan in 1967. Israeli conquest of Jerusalem in the Six Day War (June 7, 1967) fulfilled Jesus' prophecy to the letter.

Let's apply Jesus' words to Daniel's prophecy and consider how the 14,000 days project into the 21st century from Israeli conquest of Jerusalem on June 7, 1967.

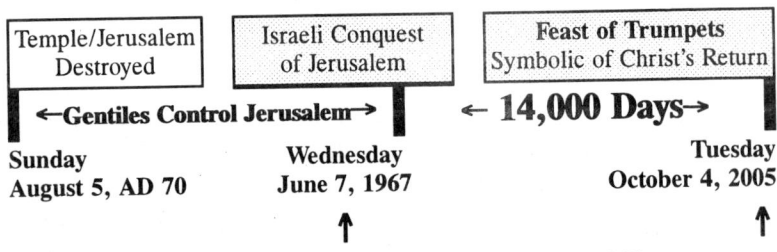

Daniel's 14,000 days point to the Feast of Trumpets, a biblical feast that hints at Christ's return. Throughout the New

Testament, the blowing of trumpets is linked to the return of Christ. In later chapters, we will discuss the impact and purpose of the Feast of Trumpets.

Signs of Deity's Intervention

My research shows how the 14,000 days point to special days like the Feast of Trumpets. The day Rome set fire to the temple was also a very special day. Let's review the impact for the day Rome burned the temple in AD 70.

Josephus tells us the temple's burning occurred twice on the same date. Jeremiah, a biblical prophet, witnessed the first burning by Babylon in 586 BC. Jeremiah recorded the date for Babylon setting fire to the temple.

> *On the **tenth day of the fifth month**, in the nineteenth year of Nebuchadnezzar king of Babylon. . . . **He set fire to the temple of the Lord**, the royal palace and all the houses of Jerusalem. Every important building he burned down* (Jer. 52:12-13).

The Romans repeated this deed in AD 70. What an amazing day Sunday, August 5, AD 70, was in terms of the divine plan for man. Two elements combine to show destiny for man. I have summarized these points as follows:

- This is the 14,000th day from Jesus' entry into Jerusalem with crowds proclaiming him to be the Messiah.
- Babylon and Rome destroyed the temple on the same date.

We can map these points as follows:

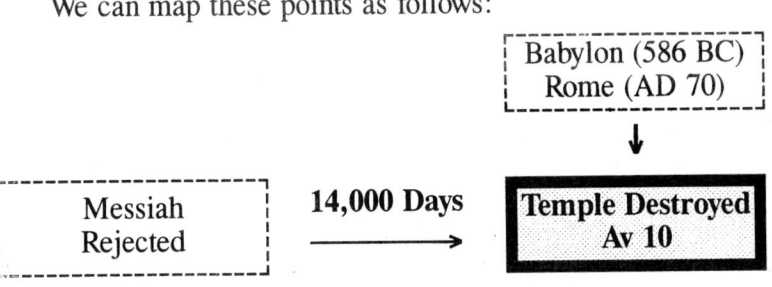

Only deity could direct human events with such precision. Daniel's 14,000 days point to a day with massive biblical implications in the 21st century, the Feast of Trumpets. Are we living in the biblical era?

Is it a coincidence to find repeatable events in man's history? Is there an intricate divine plan directing mankind?

The purpose of this chapter is to show divine intrusion in human events. Scientific dating of prophetic events reveals what appears to be the design of man's history.

END NOTES:

[a] All ancient dates will be converted to the Julian calendar. Modern dates will be Gregorian.
[b] Chart A in the back explains the Hebrew calendar
[c] Daniel's 14,000 days are counted from the end of the 69th week (Dan. 9:26) to the destruction of the temple. No time elements were given for this phase in Daniel's prophecy. The 14,000 days have been hidden until the 20th century.

Chapter 2

Separating Science from Faith

What principles support the validity of my research? This question is very important since I am examining the ethereal link between science and faith.

First and most importantly, I must stress I am surveying Scripture with science. For example, Chapter 1 shows how I used astronomy to resolve the date of the temple's ruin by Rome in AD 70. Scripture and science naturally bond together using this approach.

Another sound principle comes from using the evidence of secular (nonreligious) people. For instance, Josephus, a secular historian, recorded Jerusalem's sacking in AD 70. The link is that Daniel, a biblical prophet, foretold of Jerusalem's destruction of which Josephus was a witness.

By using science and secular writings, I can date two events in Daniel's prophecy. The two dates charted below define limits for a portion of Daniel's prophecy, which show design by counting the days between the two events.

Daniel's Prophecy Begins Persian Decree to Rebuild Jerusalem[a]	Temple set on fire[b]
Friday Mar 14, 445 BC	← 187,880 Days →	Sunday Aug 5, AD 70

13

Scientific Evidence

The time between the two events, fixed by scientific dating, is set at 187,880 days.

In Chapter 3, I will show how astronomy and archaeology pinpoint the date for rebuilding Jerusalem in 445 BC.

I cannot figure out the dates of all biblical events using science. For instance, Daniel's time line pointed to the suffering Messiah. Figuring out the date of the crucifixion requires astronomy, a secular reference, and the Bible.

Let's add the date for the Messiah's appearing at Jerusalem to the chart on the previous page.

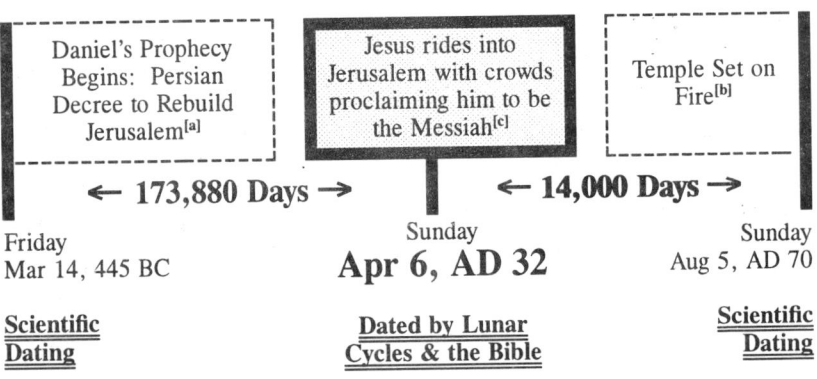

The center of the chart shows when Jesus rode into Jerusalem with crowds proclaiming him as Messiah. This divides the 187,880 days in the first chart to reveal the 14,000 days.

How did I derive this date? Sir Robert Anderson, a respected Bible scholar, initially derived the April 6, AD 32 date in 1884.[4] I have found that astronomy supports Sir Robert Anderson's AD 32 date with pinpoint accuracy. I will explain this further in Chapter 5, using biblical ideas of time gauged by astronomy.

END NOTES:
[a] Dan. 9:24-25 & Neh. 2:1-6
[b] Dan. 9:26 & Luke 21:20-24
[c] Dan. 9:25-26 & Luke 19:29-40

Chapter 3

Unraveling Prophecy With Astronomy

When Daniel was living (*c*620 to 530 BC), Jerusalem became a heap of charred ruins through Babylon's army in 586 BC. According to Daniel, the Jewish people would someday rebuild Jerusalem's ruins. A decree to reconstruct the holy city would begin a time line prophecy, pointing to the coming Messiah. Daniel wrote:

Know and understand this: ***From the issuing of the decree to restore and rebuild Jerusalem*** *until the Anointed One* [Messiah], *the ruler, comes. . .*(Dan. 9:25).

We must find the date for the decree to rebuild Jerusalem. We know that Jerusalem laid in ruins until 445 BC, the year Nehemiah discussed the plight of Jerusalem with King Artaxerxes of Persia.

³The city where my fathers are buried lies in ruins, and its gates have been destroyed by fire (Neh. 2:3b).

When Nehemiah stated his desire to rebuild Jerusalem, his request prompted King Artaxerxes to issue a decree to reconstruct the holy city.

⁴The king said to me, "What is it you want?" . . . ⁵ᵇ"Send me to the city in Judah where my fathers are buried so that I can rebuild it" (Neh. 2:1,4-5).

So Daniel foretold that a future king would issue a decree to rebuild Jerusalem. Nehemiah fulfilled Daniel's vision by recording the exact date of the decree to rebuild Jerusalem. ***<u>In the month of Nisan in the twentieth year of King Artaxerxes</u>*** *[March 14, 445 BC]* (Neh. 2:1).

How can we verify that Nehemiah received this decree from the Persian king on March 14, 445 BC?

The date recorded by Nehemiah ties directly to archaeological finds from 5th century BC Egypt. We will need to understand a little bit about astronomy since the archaeological finds reveal the positions of the moon, the earth and the sun when Nehemiah lived. Armed with astronomical facts, I can pinpoint the precise date Nehemiah received the decree to rebuild Jerusalem.

The 5th Century Before Christ

Based on Ptolemy's canon and astronomy, scholars have verified when each Persian king ruled.[5] Claudius Ptolemy (AD 70-161), a brilliant ancient scholar, assembled a precise canon with over "eighty solar, lunar and planetary positions, with their dates, which have been verified by modern astronomers."[6]

For instance, Ptolemy records that a lunar eclipse occurred in the 7th year of the Persian King Cambyses.[7][8][9] Astronomy verifies this occurred on July 16, 523 BC.

Ptolemy also recorded two lunar eclipses for the Persian King Darius. Darius' 20th and 31st years are confirmed by lunar eclipses on November 19, 502 BC[10][11] and April 25, 491 BC.[12][13][14]

These lunar eclipses verify when Cambyses and Darius ruled Persia, establishing a time line prior to Nehemiah's era. Cambyses and Darius ruled Persia according to the time line below.

Cambyses (8 Years)	Darius (36 Years)
Aug 530 BC to Jul 522 BC	Sep 522 BC to Nov 486 BC

Unraveling Prophecy With Science

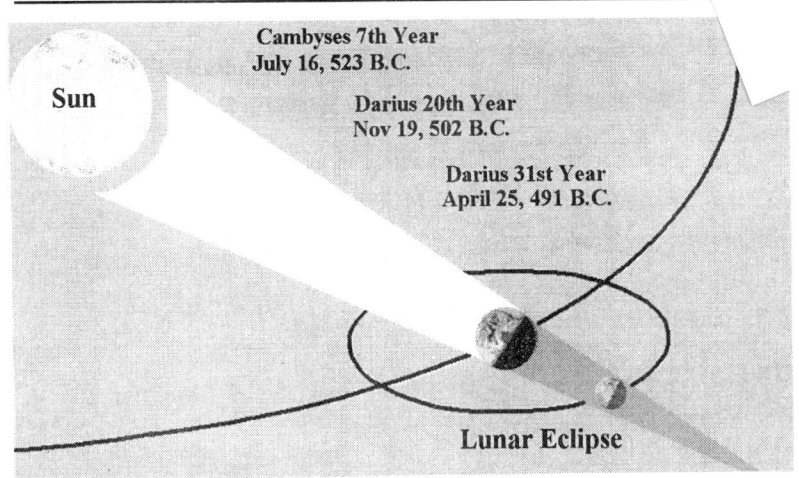

The graph above shows the lunar eclipses verifying the reigns of Cambyses and Darius. Each lunar eclipse is like a piece in a jigsaw puzzle with only one way to fit together.

King Artaxerxes - Granter of the Decree

Cambyses and Darius were followed by Xerxes and Artaxerxes. Today's scholars generally date Xerxes' and Artaxerxes' reign by the following time line:

Cambyses	Darius	Xerxes (21 Years) Nov 486 BC to Aug 465 BC	Artaxerxes (41 Years) **Aug 465 BC to 424**

The most important date in this time line is the start of King Artaxerxes' reign in August, 465 BC.

Nehemiah wrote of Artaxerxes, *"In the month of Nisan in the twentieth year of King Artaxerxes."* (Neh. 2:1). How can we find the exact date for this decree?

Egyptian archaeological discoveries from the 5th century BC hold the answer. These ancient documents contain dates for transactions such as marriages or land purchases. We can actually find out the exact day couples married 2,500 years ago by examining the texts of these papyri.

Ancient Marriage Records

Jewish scribes living in Egypt often recorded two distinct dates on legal records such as marriage papers. For example,

Scientific Evidence

scribes used an Egyptian date and a Hebrew date. We can pinpoint the exact day a couple married 2,500 years ago since the legal record had two dates. How is this possible?

Let me explain. The Egyptian date comes from the solar based Egyptian calendar, which had a 365-day year. Chart B in the back explains the Egyptian calendar.

The Hebrew date comes from the lunar based Hebrew calendar. A lunar month contains 29½ days. Twelve lunar months of 29½ days add up to 354 days in a year.

The difference between the Egyptian year (365 days) and the Hebrew year (354 days) is 11 days. This gives us a scientific method to find out when a marriage took place 2,500 years ago.

Let's illustrate how a 2,500 year old document with Egyptian and Hebrew dates can pinpoint an exact date. This also enables us to verify when King Artaxerxes reigned since each document references the year of the king's reign.

The following text comes from 5th century BC documents of the Jewish colony at Elephantine, Egypt as published by the Brooklyn Museum. I have double underlined the Egyptian date, which differs from the single underline for the Hebrew date.

> On the **25th of Phamenoth**, that is the **20th day of Siwan**, [in] the **14th year of** Artaxerxes, the king[15]

Let's convert the dates in this text to a date we can comprehend. The Egyptian solar date of Phamenoth 25 occurred on July 6 (See Chart B in the back). The Hebrew lunar date is Sivan 20. Since the first day of a lunar month happens around a new moon, we know that a new moon occurred 20 days before July 6.

These dates must match the 14th year of King Artaxerxes in the above referenced text. Artaxerxes became king in August, 465 BC. The king's 14th year could have been 452, 451 or 450 BC. I have graphed the lunar positions for each year as follows:

Unraveling Prophecy With Science

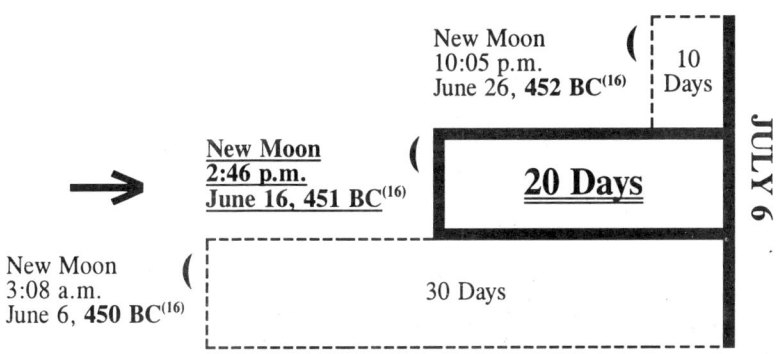

Astronomical data confirms a new moon occurred 20 days before July 6 in 451 BC.[17][18] This papyrus also confirms Artaxerxes' 14th year in 451 B.C, just like lunar eclipses prove the reigns of Cambyses and Darius.[a]

I depict the July 6, 451 BC date by the earth-moon system at the bottom of the following chart. Both the Egyptian and Hebrew calendar agree at the July 6, 451 BC date.

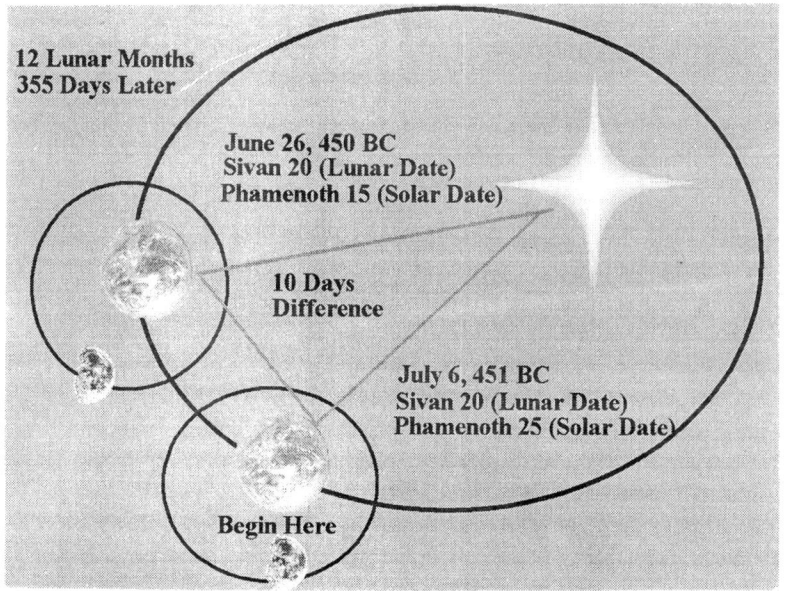

19

Scientific Evidence

One lunar year later (355 days later), the Hebrew date of Sivan 20 brings us to June 26, 450 BC, ten days short of July 6. The ten day contrast between the two calendars confirms when King Artaxerxes reigned. Astronomy, a science based on math, can find the exact date Nehemiah received the decree to rebuild Jerusalem.

Further Evidence for Nehemiah's Decree in 445 BC

Nehemiah states the decree to rebuild Jerusalem occurred on Nisan 1[19] in the 20th year of Artaxerxes. Has another ancient papyrus been unearthed that confirms Nehemiah's decree to rebuild Jerusalem on March 14, 445 BC?

Scholars date an Egyptian papyrus from the 5th century BC Jewish colony in Elephantine, Egypt on November 18, 446 BC.[20] The inscribed Hebrew date is Kislev 2, which matches the Egyptian date of Mesore 11.[b]

Kislev is the 9th Hebrew month. We can follow the sequence of Hebrew months forward from the 9th month with each succeeding new moon as follows:

Hebrew Month	Month	New Moon
Kislev	9th	November 16, 446 BC[21]
Tebeth	10th	December 15, 446 BC[21]
Shebat	11th	January 14, 445 BC[21]
Adar	12th	February 12, 445 BC[21]
NISAN	**1st**	**MARCH 13, 445 BC**[21]

This Egyptian papyrus points to March 14, 445 BC as the date cited by Nehemiah. You can read Appendix A for confirmation of this fact by astronomy and archaeology.

END NOTES:

[a] Archaeologists have numerous papyri that confirm with astronomy the reigns of Xerxes and Artaxerxes, and the biblical dates in Ezra, Nehemiah and Esther.

[b] This papyrus is Egyptian dated in the 19th year for King Artaxerxes, which turned to the 20th year on December 13. See Appendix A for clarification.

Chapter 4

Prophetic Blueprints

Does the Bible contain a blueprint that shows us when to expect divine intrusion in human affairs?

Consider that the Jewish temple burned twice on the same day of the year in history. First Babylon, then Rome more than six centuries later, set fire to the temple on the 10th day of the fifth Jewish month. This phenomenon suggests divine control of mankind.[a] Are there other examples in the Bible that might show this order?

Structure of Prophecy

Hollywood created The Ten Commandments, a movie based on the biblical story of Israel's escape from Egypt about 1450 BC. This biblical story sets up a series of events that show divine intrusion in the affairs of man.

Moses directed the Hebrews to perform unique tasks on exact days during the first Passover season. More than fourteen centuries later, Jesus followed Moses' directions to the letter. The events of Moses' era foreshadowed events in Jesus' life and ultimately converge in the 21st century. It is important we understand what these events signify before proceeding with their possible fulfillment in the 21st century.

Moses' first order for the Hebrews in Egypt was to select a lamb for the Passover on the 10th day of the first Jewish month, Nisan.

> *Tell the whole community of Israel that on the **tenth day of this month** each man is to take a lamb for his family, one for each household* (Exod. 12:3).

Scientific Evidence

What happened on this day during the Passover week at which Jesus died? Jesus purposely rode into Jerusalem on a donkey with crowds proclaiming him to be the Messiah. Jesus presented himself as the chosen Passover lamb.[b]

This picture shows the link from Moses' era to Jesus ride into Jerusalem on Nisan 10. Each picture depicts the selection of the Passover lamb.

Passover

Four days after selecting a lamb, the Hebrews killed the animal for a Passover meal. In Egypt, this took place in late afternoon on the 14th day of the month.

> *Take care of them* [the sheep] *until the **fourteenth day of the month**, when all the people of the community of Israel must slaughter them at twilight* [3:00 to 5:00 P.M]. *Then they are to take some of the blood and put it on the sides and tops of the doorframes of the houses where they eat the lambs* (Exod. 12:6-7).[c]

More than fourteen centuries later, Jesus died on the cross at the Passover. The gospel of John depicts this event taking place on the 14th day of the month.[d]

Prophetic Blueprints

The first Passover in Egypt under Moses' leadership pointed to Jesus' death on the same date.

The Resurrection

Following the Passover, the Hebrew people left Egypt and slavery. Yet, Pharaoh pursued the Hebrews with his army. Hollywood depicts these events in The Ten Commandments. A great miracle occurred when God separated the waters of the Red Sea. The Hebrews crossed the sea on dry land. However, the Egyptians drowned in the sea.

According to Moses' writings, this event occurred on Sunday[e]. Bible scholars call this the Feast of First Fruits.

*When you enter the land I am going to give you and you reap its harvest, bring to the priest a sheaf of the first grain you harvest. He is to wave the sheaf before the Lord so it will be accepted on your behalf; the priest is to wave it on the **day after the Sabbath** [the* Sunday after Passover] (Lev. 23:9-11).[f]

What happened on the corresponding Sunday after the Passover on which Jesus died? Jesus arose from the dead. Israel's supernatural deliverance from Egypt happened on the

Scientific Evidence

same day that the Messiah conquered death. The Messiah offers eternal life to anyone who truly believes.

The Apostle Paul likens Jesus' conquest of death to the Feast of First Fruits. *"Christ has indeed been raised from the dead, the **FIRSTFRUITS** of those who have fallen asleep"* (1 Cor. 15:20). Jesus could not have arose from the dead as an ordinary man.

Pentecost

Fifty days[g] after Israel's escape from Egypt, Moses received the Ten Commandments at Mount Sinai. We count the 50 days from the Feast of First Fruits.

> *From the day after the Sabbath* [Sunday], *the day you brought the sheaf of the wave offering* [First Fruits], *count off seven full weeks. Count off **fifty days** up to the **day after the seventh Sabbath** [Sunday], and then present an offering of new grain to the Lord* (Lev. 23:15-16).[h]

In the New Testament, what happened on the 50th day after Jesus arose from the dead?

> *When **the day of Pentecost** came, they* [the disciples] *were all together in one place. Suddenly a sound like the blowing of a violent wind came from heaven . . . All of them were filled with the Holy Spirit* (Acts 2:1-4).

The 50 day junction between the Old and New Testaments shows fascinating parallels. In the desert, Moses received the Ten Commandments written on stone tablets. In the New Testament, the Holy Spirit wrote the Ten Commandments on the disciples' hearts, enabling the them to love one another.

In the Old Testament story, fire descends on Mt. Sinai with the sound of voices. On the day of Pentecost, the Holy Spirit descends like fire on the disciples and enables them to speak in many different languages.

The four feasts covered so far always occur in the springtime, from late March to early June. I have summarized the four springtime feasts as follows:

Spring Feasts

Old Testament Feast	New Testament Event
Passover	Crucifixion
Unleavened Bread	Crucifixion
First Fruits	Resurrection
Pentecost	Holy Spirit

Set Dates for Divine Intrusion in Man's History

We have observed that New Testament events were fulfilled on the feast dates recorded by Moses. Did Jesus' disciples understand this link? Consider the writings of Peter.

*Concerning this salvation, the prophets, who spoke of the grace that was to come to you, searched intently and with the greatest care, trying to find out the **TIME** and **CIRCUMSTANCES** to which the Spirit of Christ in them was pointing when he predicted the **sufferings of Christ** and the glories that would follow* (1 Pet. 1:10-11).

So the prophets sought to know the time and events of the coming Messiah. The feasts give us an amazing link that direct us to watch for the return of the Messiah.

Prophetic Blueprint for the 21st Century

Biblical feasts relate to agricultural seasons. For instance, farmers begin to harvest crops in the spring and finish the harvest in autumn. Early crops such as barley and wheat are harvested in the spring. The summertime harvest includes crops like cucumbers, watermelons, and tomatoes. However, autumn brings the final harvest with great abundance.

What is the link between the agricultural seasons and the appearing of the Messiah? Jesus' first appearing occurred at the springtime harvest feasts beginning with Passover. The summertime has no biblical feasts. However, the autumn brings a new set of feasts with prophetic links. Will Jesus return to earth at the autumn feasts for the final harvest?

Scientific Evidence

The first autumn feast is called the Feast of Trumpets. Throughout the New Testament, biblical authors tie the blowing of trumpets to Christ's return. *"He will send his angels with **a loud trumpet call**, and they will gather his elect from the four winds, from one end of the heavens to the other"* (Matt. 24:31).

Since trumpets relate to Jesus coming again, what did Moses write about the Feast of Trumpets.

*On the **first day of the seventh month** you are to have a day of rest, a sacred assembly commemorated with **trumpet blasts**. Do no regular work, but present an offering made to the Lord by fire* (Lev. 23:23-25).

This verse tells us that the Feast of Trumpets occurs on the first day of the seventh Hebrew month, which is the Jewish New Year. You can find the Feast of Trumpets marked as Rosh Hashanah on your calendar. To locate Rosh Hashanah on your calendar, look for the new moon in either September or October. The Feast of Trumpets, just like Passover, is not a day that disappeared thousands of years ago.

Since trumpets relate to the return of Christ, will Jesus return to earth on the Feast of Trumpets? When Moses lived, trumpets served as alarms to awaken people for a battle. The following picture links the Feast of Trumpets to the return of Christ.

Following Christ's return on the Feast of Trumpets, a series of events will transpire on each successive autumn feast. I have projected a sequence of events by the following summary of the autumn feasts.

Autumn Feasts

Old Testament Feast	New Testament Event
Trumpets	Second Coming
Day of Atonement	Judgment
Booths	Millennial Kingdom
Booths (8th day)	Eternity

14,000 Days to the Feast of Trumpets

In Chapter 1, I gave a broad overview of my research, showing how Daniel's "time-oriented" prophecy camouflages 14,000 days from Jesus entry into Jerusalem as the Messiah to the destruction of the temple. Next, we learned that Jesus foretold of Jerusalem's destruction in AD 70, and that Jesus said Gentile nations would control Jerusalem until the time of his return. Israeli conquest of Jerusalem on June 7, 1967, fulfilled Jesus' prophecy to the letter. Israeli conquest of Jerusalem is the one sign that warns of Christ's return. My analysis then showed how Daniel's 14,000 days align to the Feast of Trumpets in the 21st century.

Israel Captures Jerusalem on June 7, 1967 (See Luke 21:7,24b)	**Feast of Trumpets** **Christ's Return** **October 4, 2005**

14,000 Days
Israeli Conquest of Jerusalem to the Feast of Trumpets

Are the 14,000 days and the Feast of Trumpets just an anomaly of history?[i]

Scientific Evidence

Daniel

Daniel was a legend in his time. In Babylon, Daniel decoded dreams and received revelation from angelic beings. When Daniel grew old, he was lauded by the queen of Babylon. *"There is a man [Daniel] in your kingdom who has the spirit of the holy gods in him. In the time of your father he was found to have insight and intelligence and wisdom like that of the gods"* (Dan. 5:11).

Both Moses and Daniel received revelation from God about the time of the suffering Messiah. Daniel wrote of the suffering Messiah. *"the Anointed One [Messiah] will be cut off [crucified] and will have nothing"* (Dan. 9:26).

I have discovered how Moses' and Daniel's prophecies coincide at prophetic events. For instance, I have shown how Jesus fulfilled the Passover feasts of which Moses penned. Now we will see how Daniel's "time-oriented" prophecy pointed to the Passover season at which Jesus died.

Pinpoint Accuracy

The springtime feasts happen every year, meaning the feasts occur in cycles. We can graph cyclical events such as the Passover for the years AD 29 to 33 as follows:

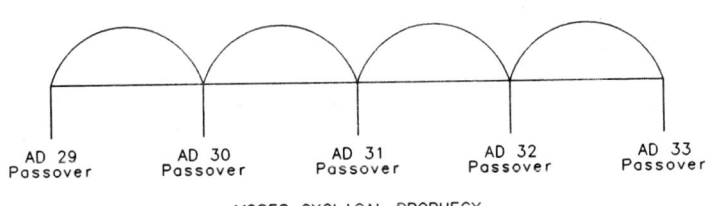

MOSES CYCLICAL PROPHECY

Cyclical events, such as the Passover, do not pinpoint when the Messiah will appear. The suffering Messiah could have appeared at any of numerous Passovers. However, the

Prophetic Blueprints

coinciding of Moses' cyclical feasts with Daniel's linear prophecy reveal when the Messiah will appear.

Let me explain what linear prophecy means. Linear means to draw a straight line on a piece of paper. On the left side of the line, write the word "beginning." On the right side of the line, write the word "ending."

Daniel's prophecies are linear. Linear prophecies happen only once with a beginning and ending point. I have mapped Daniel's linear prophecy to Moses' cyclical prophecies, showing how both prophecies coincided at Jesus' suffering in AD 32.

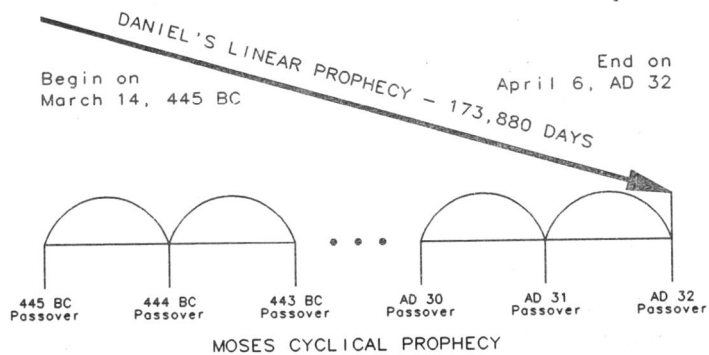

On the left side of the graph above, Daniel's linear prophecy began on March 14, 445 BC. On the right side, Daniel's time line pointed to Jesus' entry into Jerusalem on Sunday, April 6, AD 32. Lunar cycles will verify this date with amazing accuracy in Chapter 5.

END NOTES:

[a] Read Amos 3:2 based on the fact that the temple burned down on exact days in history.

[b] See John 12:1-16: Jesus went to Bethany, a city east of Jerusalem, on Nisan 8. On Nisan 9, Mary, Martha & Lazarus were present for a special meal. On Nisan 10, Jesus rode into Jerusalem. (See Luke 19:29-44 also).

[c] Also see Lev. 23:5

[d] John 18:28,39 & John 19:14: Matthew, Mark & Luke depict Jesus' crucifixion on Nisan 15, a day later.

[e] The exact dates for events at the first Passover can be correlated between the stories in Exodus and Moses' writings in Leviticus 23. So the events and dates for Israel's escape from Egypt were later codified in Leviticus.

[f] Also, see the story of Israel crossing the Red Sea in Exod. 12:37 - 14:31.

[g] See Exod. 19:1, Israel camped at Mt. Sinai on the 3rd day of the 3rd month [Sivan 3]. Moses probably ascended Mt. Sinai on Sivan 4. Exod. 19:3 to 20:17 portrays the law being given on the third day. Tradition says that Moses received the Ten Commandments on Sivan 6. Fifty days are counted from Nisan 18 (crossing the red sea) to Sivan 6.

[h] Also, you can read about Moses receiving the law in Exod. 19:1-17.

[i] Perhaps you will want to learn more about the Bible. "Preparations" in the back is for your benefit.

Chapter 5

The First Coming: A Lunar Appraisal

I have used scientific dating to pinpoint the day Daniel's "time-oriented" prophecy began and the day Rome set fire to the temple. The left and right side of the chart below, marked with dashed lines, show these dates.

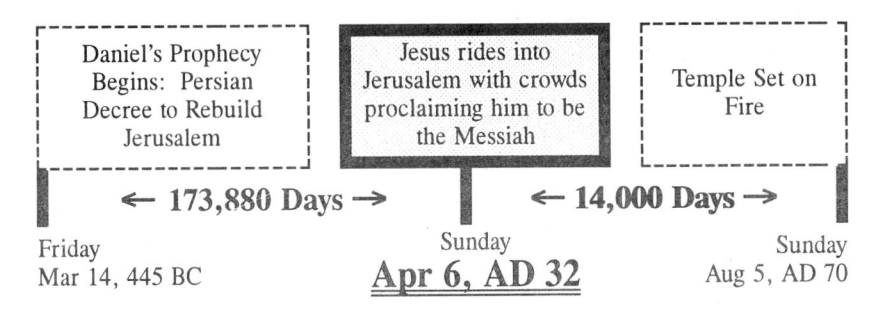

Daniel's Prophecy Begins: Persian Decree to Rebuild Jerusalem	Jesus rides into Jerusalem with crowds proclaiming him to be the Messiah	Temple Set on Fire
← 173,880 Days →		← 14,000 Days →
Friday Mar 14, 445 BC	Sunday **Apr 6, AD 32**	Sunday Aug 5, AD 70

The middle of the summary above shows the date Jesus entered Jerusalem before his crucifixion. Pinpointing the date on which Jesus rode into Jerusalem is pivotal since it exposes the 14,000 days hidden in Daniel's linear prophecy. I will use both astronomy and the Bible to pinpoint this date.

How can I verify that Jesus died in AD 32?

I will use a method similar to how I pinpointed the day Rome set fire to the temple in AD 70. For instance, I pinpointed the temple's destruction on August 5, AD 70, because I knew the day of the week (Sunday), the year (AD 70), and the 50 day time length from the temple's destruction to the Jewish New Year.

Scientific Evidence

Figuring out the date of Jesus' crucifixion requires the same kind of information. For instance, we must find out the day of the week on which Jesus died and the most likely years for the crucifixion. Finally, I will show how the moon's orbit about the earth isolates the AD 32 date.

Biblical Date of the Crucifixion

The gospel of John differs with Matthew, Mark and Luke for the biblical date of the crucifixion. According to John's gospel, Jesus died on Nisan 14, the Passover. However, Matthew, Mark and Luke declare that Jesus died on Nisan 15, the Feast of Unleavened Bread.[a]

I have chosen to agree with Matthew, Mark, and Luke for a Nisan 15 date for Jesus' crucifixion. I base my choice on the fact that Matthew, Mark and Luke wrote their gospels many decades before John. John wrote about Jesus near the end of the first century to confront false teachings about Jesus.

Perhaps more importantly, astronomical data supports the historic setting found in Matthew, Mark and Luke over the gospel of John.[b] However, I cannot give the astronomical facts until the end of this chapter and Appendix C. Let's begin by finding out the day of the week on which Jesus died.

Day of the Crucifixion

According to the gospels, Jesus arose from the dead on Sunday, the third day after the crucifixion. All of Christendom accepts that Jesus resurrected on Sunday. Since Jesus died three days before Sunday, we must understand how biblical people counted three days at the time of Moses or Jesus.

In our culture, if I said "Let's meet in three days," we would count tomorrow as the first day. Contrary to our society, the biblical culture counts today as the first day. Consider how each day is counted in the following Scripture.

The First Coming: A Lunar Appraisal

*When you sacrifice a fellowship offering to the Lord, sacrifice it in such a way that it will be accepted on your behalf. It shall be eaten on **the day you sacrifice it** [1st Day] or on the **next day** [2nd Day]; anything left over **until the third day** [3rd Day] must be burned up. If any of it is eaten on the third day, it is impure and will not be accepted* (Lev. 19:5-7).

How are the three days counted in this verse? Consider how the first day is counted by these two points:

- Today, the day of the sacrifice, counts as the first day.
- Today counts as a whole day, not part of a day.

We have found a 24-hour contrast between the way our culture counts three days versus the biblical culture. In the verse above, the only full 24-hour day is the second day. Finally, the third day, a partial day, counts as a whole day. We can map this method of counting as follows:

Partial Day	24-Hour Day	Partial Day
First Day	Second Day	Third Day

Applying this verse to Jesus' crucifixion, we realize that the day of Jesus' death, Friday, counted as the first day. The only full 24-hour day was Saturday. Jesus' Sunday resurrection, a partial day, counted as the third day.[c]

(1) Jesus died on a Friday

I will highlight time related ideas for dating the crucifixion with dark lines as shown above. The **(1)** notation on the left side of the chart above is the first of three conclusions required to date the crucifixion. If you want more information to clarify that Jesus died on Friday, please read Appendix B.

Scientific Evidence

Historic Setting of the Crucifixion

Scholars have verified that the temple was destroyed by Rome in AD 70. By knowing the year of the temple's burning, I easily found the date of that event. However, the crucifixion has several years that could qualify as the year Jesus died. We know the year Jesus began his ministry since Luke specifies the year Jesus went to the river Jordan to be baptized by John the Baptist.

In the fifteenth year of the reign of Tiberias Caesar (Luke 3:1).

Tiberias Caesar became emperor of Rome on August 19, AD 14. By counting the years for Tiberias' reign, we know his 15th year began on August 19, AD 28, and ended one year later. Jesus began his ministry in this interval.

What can we learn from Jesus being baptized in the 15th year of Tiberias Caesar? We can discover when Jesus' first Passover occurred. There are two possible years. If John baptized Jesus before the Passover in AD 29, then Jesus' first recorded Passover happened in AD 29.

Aug 19, AD 28 Tiberias' 15th Year Begins	Baptized Before Passover AD	Passover AD 29

However, if Jesus were baptized after the Passover in AD 29, then his first Passover would have been in AD 30.

Jesus' first Passover occurred in AD 29 or 30

We have set the beginning years of Jesus' ministry. If we add the number of years Jesus' ministry lasted to AD 29 or 30, then we can find the most viable years for the crucifixion. John's gospel refers to three or possibly four Passovers during Jesus' ministry.[d] We simply add three to four years to AD 29 or 30, the year Jesus began his ministry, to find viable years for the crucifixion.

The First Coming: A Lunar Appraisal

If Jesus' first Passover happened in AD 29, and we add three or four Passover years, then Jesus died at either the Passover in AD 31 or 32 as follows:

AD 29	AD 30	AD 31	AD 32
1st Passover	2nd Passover	**3rd Passover**	**4th Passover**

What is the latest year possible for Jesus' death? Jesus' first Passover may have happened in AD 30. If we add four Passover years to AD 30, then Jesus died at the Passover in AD 33 as follows:

AD 30	AD 31	AD 32	AD 33
1st Passover	2nd Passover	3rd Passover	**4th Passover**

Based on the gospels of Luke and John, the primary years for Jesus' crucifixion had to be AD 31, 32 or 33.[22]

> **(2) Jesus died on the Passover in either AD 31, 32 or 33**

Daniel's Linear Prophecy and Lunar Cycles

In Chapter 3 and Appendix A, I used astronomy and archaeology to show Daniel's linear prophecy began on March 14, 445 BC. We count 173,880 days from March 14, 445 BC, to Jesus' entry into Jerusalem on April 6, AD 32.

Daniel's Prophecy Begins	Jesus rides into Jerusalem
Jerusalem to be Rebuilt	as the Messiah
Friday, Mar 14, 445 BC	Sunday, Apr 6, AD 32

⟵ **173,880 Days** ⟶

Why are the 173,880 days important?

35

Scientific Evidence

In AD 70, I showed a time length of 50 days for finding the date of the temple's burning. The 173,880 days, like the 50 day time length in AD 70, give us a time length that is vital to finding the date of Jesus' death.

The 173,880 days come from Daniel's prophecy. Let's review the "time-oriented" verses.

> *From the issuing of the decree to restore and rebuild Jerusalem until the Anointed One* [Messiah], *the ruler, comes, there will be* <u>*seven 'sevens,'*</u> *and* <u>*sixty-two 'sevens.'*</u> *.... After the sixty-two 'sevens,' the Anointed One will be cut off* [crucified] *and will have nothing* (Dan. 9:25-26).

How do we get 173,880 days from Daniel's "time-oriented" prophecy? To begin, we must find out what "seven 'sevens'" mean. In the original language, the word for "sevens" means a period of seven years.[23] Therefore, we simply multiply 7 x 7 to equal 49 years as follows:

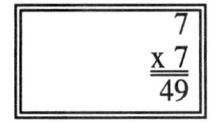

$$\begin{array}{r} 7 \\ \times\ 7 \\ \hline 49 \end{array}$$

Daniel also gives us a period of sixty-two 'sevens.' We multiply 62 x 7 to equal 434 years as follows:

$$\begin{array}{r} 7 \\ \times\ 62 \\ \hline 434 \end{array}$$

Since the 49 years are followed by 434 years, we must add the two numbers to total 483 years as follows:

$$\begin{array}{r} 49 \\ +\ 434 \\ \hline 483 \end{array}$$

The First Coming: A Lunar Appraisal

What is the purpose of these numbers? Daniel's numbers give us a time line from the decree to rebuild Jerusalem to the day Jesus would enter the holy city as the Messiah.

If we convert the 483 years into days, we get 173,880 days. This will show the extreme accuracy of Daniel's "time-oriented" prophecy.

Let's multiply the 483 years by the number of days in a year. Our solar calendar has 365¼ days each year. The Hebrew lunar calendar contains 354 days in a normal year or 383 days in a leap year. Which length is correct? We must use the length of a year revealed in the Bible.

The Bible uses 360 days for a biblical year. We find the 360 days in the books of Genesis[e] and Revelation. Let's consider the 360-day year found in the book of Revelation.

> *They* [Gentiles] *will trample on the holy city for **42 months**. And I will give power to my two witnesses, and they will prophesy for **1,260 days**, clothed in sackcloth* (Rev. 11:2-3).

By this verse, 1,260 days equal 42 months. We divide the 1,260 days by 42 months to arrive at 30 days in a month as follows:

$$\frac{1,260}{42} = 30$$

Since there are 12 months in a year, we multiply 30 x 12 to equal 360 days in a year as follows:

$$30 \times 12 = 360$$

Now we can get the exact length of Daniel's time line. We must multiply 483 years by 360 days in a year to get 173,880 days.

Scientific Evidence

$$360 \times 483 = 173{,}880$$

When we add 173,880 days to March 14, 445 BC, we arrive at Sunday, April 6, AD 32. Jesus rode into Jerusalem on this day with crowds proclaiming him as the Messiah.

Lunar Cycles

We have seen that Daniel's prophecy was fulfilled to the very day, and it is incredibly accurate. Is the 360-day year interpretation of Daniel and the 173,880 days correct? Let's analyze the approach using astronomy.

Before we use astronomy, we must note the lunar position when Daniel's time line began and ended. For instance, when Nehemiah received the decree to rebuild Jerusalem, a new moon hung in the sky. It was Nisan 1. This picture shows the lunar position for the Hebrew date of Nisan 1 (See Chapter 3).

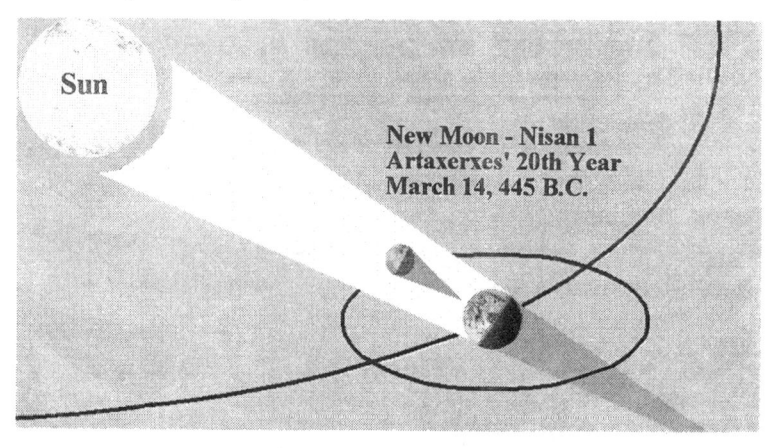

Daniel's time line prophecy ended when Jesus rode into Jerusalem with crowds proclaiming him as the Messiah on Nisan 10 (see Chapter 4). The moon circled the earth 5,888 times from the decree given to Nehemiah to rebuild Jerusalem to the day Jesus rode into Jerusalem as the Messiah, and

The First Coming: A Lunar Appraisal

had moved nine days past the new moon position to Nisan 10 as shown below.

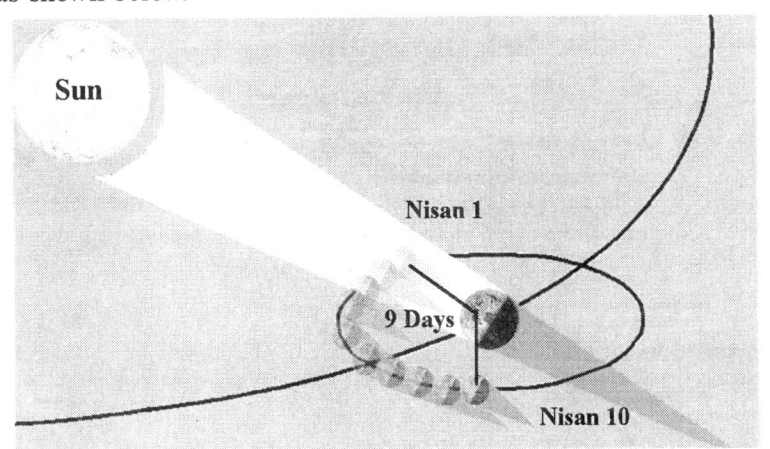

The previous graphs show the lunar position at the beginning (Nisan 1) and ending (Nisan 10) points of Daniel's prophecy. I can now analyze the 173,880 days with lunar cycles. How many revolutions did the moon make around the earth in 173,880 days. I find the answer by dividing the 173,880 days by the time it takes the moon to circle the earth.

The moon circles the earth every 29½ days. The exact time is 29 days, 12 hours, 44 minutes, and 2.8 seconds. The division gives the following answer.

$$\frac{173,880}{29\frac{1}{2}} = 5,888 \text{ Revolutions} + 3.9 \text{ Days Leftover}$$

The moon circled the earth 5,888 times with a remainder of 3.9 days. The 5,888 lunar circuits started on Nisan 1, the new moon in Nehemiah's era and end on Nisan 1, the new moon in Jesus' era. But, there are only 3.9 days remaining.

Since we are dealing with the calendar, the remainder of 3.9 days equal four complete days. Adding the four days to Nisan 1 brings us to Nisan 5. But the end of Daniel's time line is Nisan 10. We have a problem. The picture below shows how the lunar position lacks five complete days.

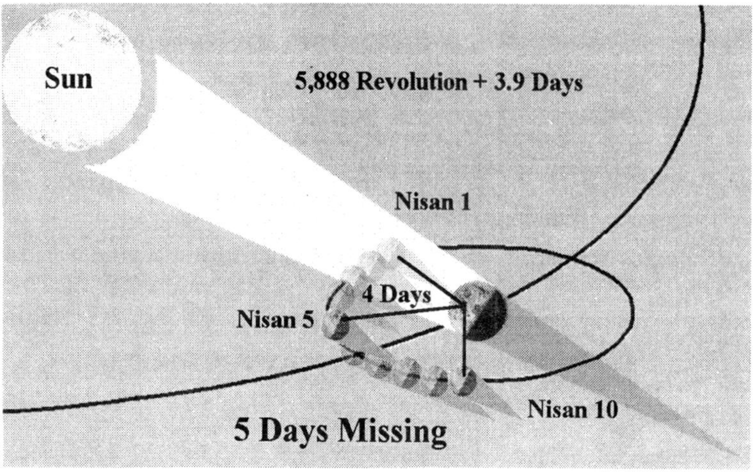
Sun
5,888 Revolution + 3.9 Days
Nisan 1
4 Days
Nisan 5
Nisan 10
5 Days Missing

The graph shows five missing days from Nisan 5 to Nisan 10. How can I account for the five missing days?

The Solution

Finding the five missing days requires me to move the problem forward to the full moon on Nisan 15, the date of the crucifixion. Since there are five days missing at Nisan 10, there will also be five days missing at the full moon on Nisan 15. The following chart shows where the full moon should be for the Friday crucifixion, with five missing days.

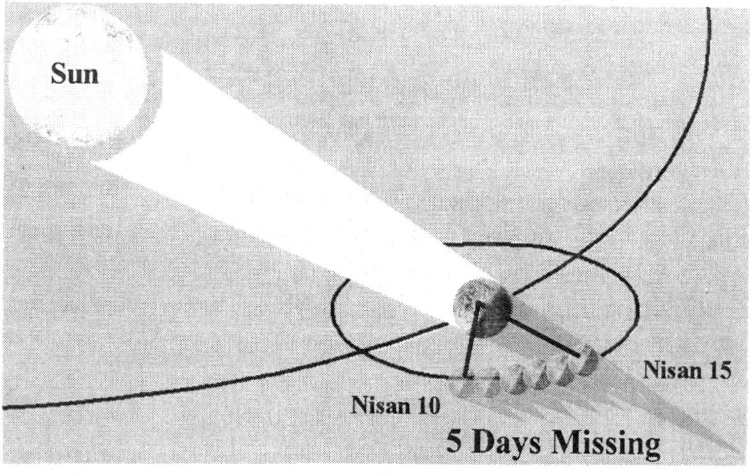
Sun
Nisan 15
Nisan 10
5 Days Missing

The First Coming: A Lunar Appraisal

The ideal lunar alignment for the crucifixion would have the moon in line with the earth and sun on Nisan 15, a Friday. However, the five missing days illustrate an important question. Did the crucifixion occur on a Friday with a full moon? Many scholars[24][25] and scientists[26] have assumed that Jesus died on a Friday with a full moon. Yet, the five missing days reveal the fault of the full moon on a Friday assumption.

The 173,880 days from Daniel point to AD 32 as the year of Jesus' crucifixion. Astronomical charts for AD 32 show the full moon did not occur until Monday, April 14, about noon time. Since Jesus would have died on Friday, April 11, the astronomical charts uncover three missing days in the year AD 32. You can count the three days from Friday, the day of Jesus' death, to the full moon on Monday as follows:

Full Moon ●
at 12:06 p.m.[27]

	24 Hours	48 Hours	72 Hours After Jesus' Death
Friday Crucifixion	Saturday	Sunday	Monday

This accounts for three of the five missing days.[f]

Where do I find the other two missing days? The only place to look for the missing days is at the start of Daniel's prophecy in 445 BC. Astronomical charts show the new moon occurred at 7:12 a.m. on March 13, 445 BC.[30] But, the decree to rebuild Jerusalem happened one day later on March 14. This accounts for another missing day. Where is the other missing day?

Earlier in this chapter, we learned the biblical method for counting days showing the first day, a partial day, counts as day number one.[g] The biblical method of counting days uncovers the fifth missing day.

41

Scientific Evidence

We have learned two important facts by probing Daniel's time line with lunar cycles.

- The Hebrew calendar was off by three days in AD 32.[h]
- The crucifixion had to occur **BEFORE** a full moon.

The picture below shows the lunar position on the day Jesus died and where the four missing days are found.

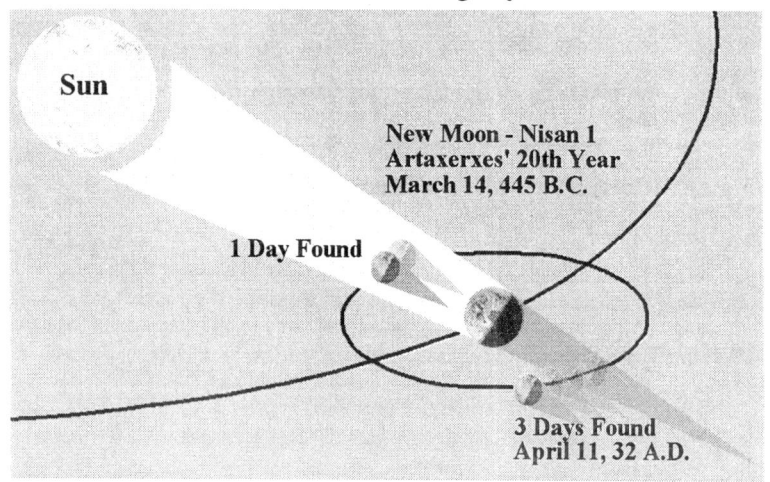

Sun

New Moon - Nisan 1
Artaxerxes' 20th Year
March 14, 445 B.C.

1 Day Found

3 Days Found
April 11, 32 A.D.

> **(3)** In the year of the crucifixion, a full moon occurred three days after Jesus died.

Daniel's prophecy was fulfilled to the very day with amazing accuracy. Astronomical charts support the biblical 360-day year interpretation of Daniel's time line. Appendix D discusses the 360-day year and other views of Daniel.

The 360-day year interpretation of Daniel exposes the 14,000 days from Jesus' ride into Jerusalem as the Messiah to the temple's destruction in AD 70. Scientific dating of biblical events appears to show divine influence in human events. Was God directing Israeli conquest of Jerusalem in the Six Day War to align the 14,000 days perfectly with the Feast of Trumpets in 2005? Is it possible that Daniel's prophecy and

The First Coming: A Lunar Appraisal

the Messiah's utterances are unfolding with divine perfection for modern man?[i]

Do you want more information on dating the crucifixion? Appendix C completes the astronomical analysis, showing results for the years AD 29 to 34. I suggest you read Appendix C while the concepts in Chapter 5 are fresh, then return to Chapter 6.

END NOTES:

[a] The distinct dates for the crucifixion are noted as follows:

Nisan 14	**Nisan 15**
Passover Lamb Slaughtered	Firstborn in Egypt Die
• Exod. 12:6-7	• Exod. 12:8-13, 29-30
• Lev. 23:5	• Lev. 23:6-8
	• Matt 26:17-20
• John 18:28,39	• Mark 14:12-17
• John 19:14,31	• Luke 22:7-15

[b] John's gospel is an integral part of God's revelation to man. I hold John's gospel of high esteem.

[c] Other biblical references.
- Scriptures for counting three days (Lev. 7:16-18; Exod. 19:10-11, 16; Esth. 4:16-5:1).
- Luke depicts a partial day, Sunday, as the third day (Luke 24:1-3, 13-16, 21).
- Lev. 23:15-16: Pentecost is 50 days, yet by modern counting methods there are only 49 days.
- In 1 Cor. 15:3-6, Paul says that Christ was "raised on the third day according to the Scriptures." portraying that part of a day counts as a whole day. Moreover, this is "according to the Scriptures," meaning the verses in Lev. 7:16-18 & 19:5-7.

[d] See John 2:13, 5:1 (implied), 6:4 and Chapters 18 and 19 at which the crucifixion occurred.

Scientific Evidence

[e] Gen. 7:11 & 8:3-4: 150 days in five months = 30 days/month; Hence, 12 x 30 = 360 days/year.

[f] In the year AD 32, Nisan 10 was actually off by three full days relative to the lunar position. Stated another way, Nisan 10 should have been Nisan 7. The Hebrew calendar is only an approximation of the moon's position relative to the earth. Our solar calendar is also an approximation of the earth's position relative to the sun. Scholars have shown that the religious calendar of Jerusalem could be off by three full days.[28][29]

[g] When we divided the 173,880 days by one lunar cycle, we were counting full 24-hour days. When the biblical method of counting days is applied, we must subtract one day from the 173,880 days to have full 24-hour days. In other words, the astronomical method for counting requires us to use 173,879 days.[31] Therefore, the partial day is eliminated.

[h] Before AD 360, the Hebrew calendar varied up to five days annually with lengths of 352 to 356 days. The five day variation allowed up to three days divergence either before or after the exact time of the new moon. My research, based on astronomical charts and the biblical story, shows a three day discrepancy for AD 32, a very rare occurrence. How was the first day of each month set in the first century? A court required witnesses to agree through observing each new crescent. According to Encyclopedia Judaica, fixing the first day of a new month could be deliberately prolonged or sped up by choosing a site favorable for observing the new crescent. My research agrees with Encyclopedia Judaica.[29]

[i] Should you want to learn more about the Bible, "Preparations" in the back is for your benefit.

Chapter 6

Christ's Return
The Lunar Junction

What an amazing story evolves by using astronomy to find the dates of prophetic events. A clear message shows the hand of providence in human events.

Did Moses and Daniel understand that they could foresee the time and events of the Messiah's coming? Although Moses and Daniel did not comprehend everything, they knew God intimately and talked with Him. Through Moses and Daniel, God foretold the exact time and events of Jesus' first appearing. Did Moses and Daniel receive divine knowledge about the time and events of Christ's return?

My research, based on Moses and Daniel, shows that 14,000 days passed from the day Jesus entered Jerusalem as the Messiah to the day Rome set fire to the temple. What did Jesus say about the temple's future destruction in AD 70?

A few days before the crucifixion, Jesus listened to the disciples brag about the beauty of the temple. However, Jesus told his disciples that the temple would be destroyed. Intrigued by Jesus' words, the disciples asked him about the temple's destruction. *"**When** will these things happen? And **what** will be the sign [one sign] that they are about to take place?"* (Luke 21:7).

It is important to note that the disciples asked only about the temple's future destruction. Yet, Jesus gave an answer that

Scientific Evidence

linked the temple's destruction to his return. Jesus foretold, *"Jerusalem will be trampled on by the Gentiles until the times of the Gentiles are fulfilled"* (Luke 21:24b).

So Jesus foretold of Jerusalem's destruction in AD 70, then of Israeli conquest of the holy city on June 7, 1967. First the Jewish people lose Jerusalem, then the Jewish people regain Jerusalem. So one principle connects these two historic events, the Jewish people controlling Jerusalem.

Next, Jesus linked Israeli conquest of Jerusalem on June 7, 1967, to a final generation. Jesus said, *"I tell you the truth, this generation will certainly not pass away until all these things have happened"* (Luke 21:32).

What is the length of the final generation? Since Jesus linked his return to the temple's destruction in AD 70, could it be possible that the 14,000 days of Daniel measure the length of parallel generations? Are we looking at a repeat of biblical events in the 21st century?

In Chapter 4, I showed how Daniel's linear prophecy points directly to Moses' cyclical prophecies. The link between the two prophets is perfect for the 21st century.

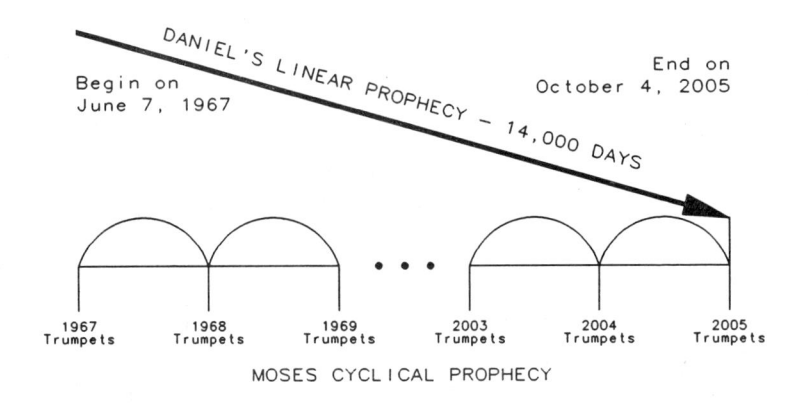

DANIEL'S LINEAR PROPHECY – 14,000 DAYS

Begin on June 7, 1967

End on October 4, 2005

1967 Trumpets
1968 Trumpets
1969 Trumpets
2003 Trumpets
2004 Trumpets
2005 Trumpets

MOSES CYCLICAL PROPHECY

Christ's Return: The Lunar Junction

Is it a coincidence to find the 14,000 days of Jesus' era fit perfectly to the Feast of Trumpets in the 21st century? Did humanity witness providence moving in human events when Israel retook Jerusalem on June 7, 1967?

The Method and Rule for Interpretation

I have used scientific dating as a method to interpret Daniel's linear prophecy. By fixing exact dates for prophetic events, Daniel's mysterious prophecy is clarified.

My rule for interpreting Daniel's "time-oriented" prophecy comes from the prophecy itself. Daniel was praying about the Hebrew people returning to Jerusalem when an angel appeared. The angel told Daniel that the prophecy is "*decreed for your people* [the Jewish people] *and your holy city* [Jerusalem]" (Dan. 9:24). Therefore, the rule for solving the prophecy is the "**Jewish people controlling Jerusalem**."[32] Jesus' continued with this principle when he foretold of Jerusalem's future. We can map this rule from our view of history as follows:

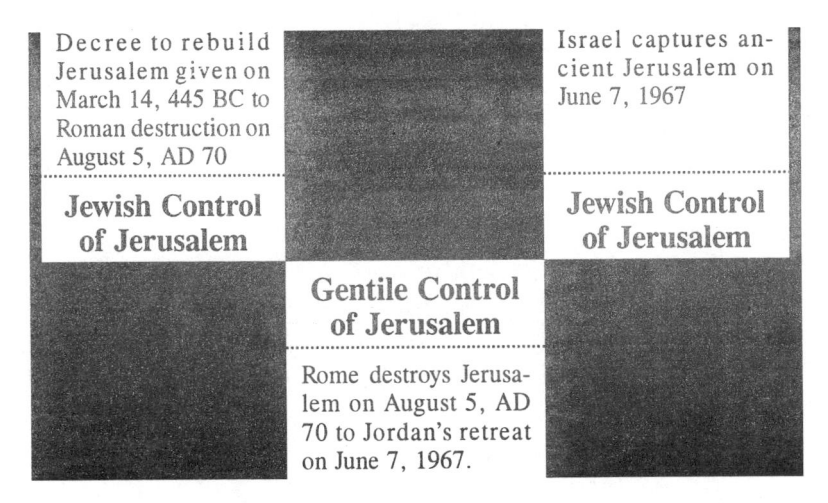

Decree to rebuild Jerusalem given on March 14, 445 BC to Roman destruction on August 5, AD 70		Israel captures ancient Jerusalem on June 7, 1967
Jewish Control of Jerusalem		**Jewish Control of Jerusalem**
	Gentile Control of Jerusalem	
	Rome destroys Jerusalem on August 5, AD 70 to Jordan's retreat on June 7, 1967.	

We can see how the Hebrews began to control Jerusalem in 445 BC. Jerusalem's ruin by the Romans in AD 70 ended Jewish control of the holy city.

Scientific Evidence

Gentiles nations, including Christians and Muslims[a], governed Jerusalem from AD 70 to 1967. Jesus' words clarify this phase of Gentile control as follows:

Jerusalem will be trampled on by the Gentiles until the times of the Gentiles are fulfilled (Luke 21:24b).

This verse covers 1,897 years, noted by the middle of the chart above. Daniel foretold of Jerusalem's ruin by the Romans in AD 70.[b] Yet, Daniel's time line for Jerusalem did not specify a time duration for Gentile control of Jerusalem. Jesus' words about Gentile control of Jerusalem fill a vacuum in Daniel's "time-oriented" prophecy, bringing the time line into the 20th century.[33]

Israeli conquest of Jerusalem on June 7, 1967, renewed Jewish control of the holy city. This also restored the rule for decoding Daniel's time line and is the specific sign of Christ's return in Luke's gospel.[34]

Daniel's 14,000 days show man's destiny. Time is counting down to the lunar junction on October 4, 2005, a new moon feast.[c] Scientific dating of "time-oriented" Scripture asserts that the whole world will know the day of Christ's return. If this is true, what did Jesus mean by saying *"No one knows about that day or hour"* (Matt. 24:36).

END NOTES:

[a] Muslims believe that their control of Jerusalem across the centuries proved Islam to be superior to Christianity and Judaism.[35] However, Islam's validity is confronted by Israeli conquest of Jerusalem on June 7, 1967, which aligns the 14,000 days to the Feast of Trumpets. Islam will cease to be a religion at Christ's return (See Isa. 19:21-25). If you believe in the tenets of Islam or Judaism, I suggest you order the free literature available in the back section entitled "Preparations".

[b] Dan. 9:26

[c] See Col. 2:17-18

Chapter 7

The Unknown Factor

What an incredible discovery to find parallel 14,000 day generations at the time of Christ and for our time. Since there is a perfect aligning of the 14,000 days to the Feast of Trumpets on October 4, 2005, what did Jesus mean by saying:

> *[36]No one knows about that day or hour, not even the angels in heaven, nor the Son, but only the Father. [37]As it was in the days of Noah, so it will be at the coming of the Son of Man. [38]For in the days before the flood, people were eating and drinking, marrying and giving in marriage, up to the day Noah entered the ark; [39]and they knew nothing about what would happen until the flood came and took them all away. That is how it will be at the coming of the Son of Man. [40]Two men will be in the field; one will be taken and the other left. [41]Two women will be grinding with a hand mill; one will be taken and the other left* (Matt. 24:36-41).

Let's consider the context of Jesus' words following his statement that nobody would know the day or hour of the Messiah's return. Verses 37 through 39 teach us that at the time of Christ's coming, life will be going on in a normal fashion. People will be marrying and raising families. The economy will be operating in its normal up and down cycles. Everyday life will be normal. Yet, verses 40 through 41 teach us that a separation of people suddenly takes place. One person will vanish, leaving the other person in despair.

Scientific Evidence

What can we learn about the day and hour no one knows? The day and hour that no one can know is the separation of believers from non-believers. Christians call the day of separation, ***The Rapture.*** True followers of Christ will suddenly depart. The apocalypse of which Scripture foretells will fall on the people left behind on earth.

The Known Day

The theory of 14,000 days points to a known day, the Feast of Trumpets. Is there a Scripture that would support a known day for Christ's return? Consider Daniel's words.

From the time that the daily sacrifice is abolished and the abomination that causes desolation is set up, there will be 1,290 days. ***Blessed is the one who waits for and reaches the end of the 1,335 days*** (Dan. 12:11-12).

According to Daniel,[a] people who witness the stopping of the daily sacrifice at the temple in Jerusalem can count down to a known day 1,335 days later, the return of Christ. The Scriptures seem to support an unknown day and hour for Christ's return, and a known day is also possible.

We can map the unknown day and known day of Christ's appearing by the following chart:

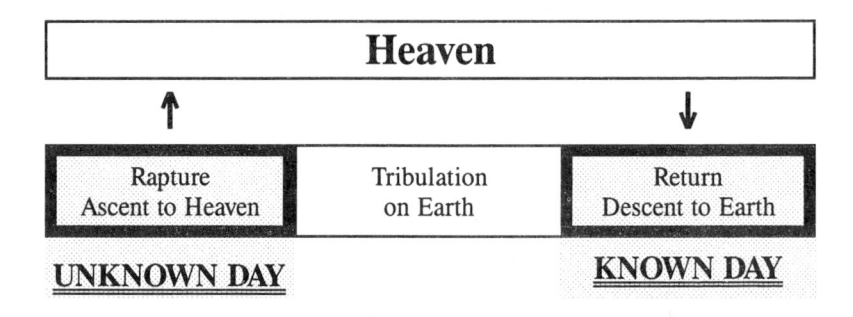

Heaven		
↑		↓
Rapture Ascent to Heaven	Tribulation on Earth	Return Descent to Earth
UNKNOWN DAY		**KNOWN DAY**

The left side of this chart depicts Christians ascending to heaven, the unknown day. The right side of the chart depicts the return of Christ, the known day of which Daniel foretells.

The Rapture in Scripture

I have written *Scientific Evidence for the Second Coming of Christ* as a supplement to *Threshold of Eternity*. In this book, I don't have space to adequately discuss the rapture. Should you want to learn more, you can order a book packed with details about your future.

☑ *<u>Mysterious Numbers of the Sealed Revelation</u>*

- Unlocks the mystery of Daniel's sealed visions
- Discusses intriguing information about the rapture

Read Appendix D for more details about this book. Also, I am producing a monthly newsletter, **The Cutting Edge,** for people who want to keep in contact and learn how prophetic studies are for evangelism. These items can be ordered in the back section entitled "Preparations".

END NOTES:

[a] Jesus spoke of Daniel's abomination of desolation, calling it the **<u>one sign</u>** that marks the "end of the age." Compare Matt. 24:3,15 to Dan. 12:11-12

Appendix A

The Reign of Artaxerxes

Xerxes, the father of Artaxerxes, was murdered by political aids in August, 465 BC. Scribes recorded Xerxes' assassination date on a clay tablet known as a Babylonian Astronomical Text. Scholars[36][37] have translated the text, showing the murder occurred between August 4 to 18, 465 BC.[38] Upon his father's death, Artaxerxes became king of Persia.

Scholars use the Babylonian Astronomical Text to establish August, 465 BC, as the first month of Artaxerxes' reign. Egyptian papyri also support Artaxerxes' ascent to power in August, 465 BC, with astronomy. I will show this evidence after explaining how the years of a king's reign were counted in the 5th century BC.

How the Years of a King's Reign Were Counted

The Hebrews, Babylonians and Egyptians used a common principle for counting the years of a king's reign in the 5th century BC. The year that a new king came to power was called the year of the king's ascension, which ended the day before New Year's Day.

Each of the three cultures observed New Year's Day at a different time of the year. In the 5th century BC, New Year's Day for each culture occurred in the following sequence after Artaxerxes became king in August, 465 BC.

Hebrew[39]	Tishri 1 (September - October)
Egypt[40]	Thoth 1 (December)
Babylon	Nisanu 1 (March - April)

After Artaxerxes became king, the Hebrews were the first to observe New Year's Day on October 17, 465 BC,[41][42] By the Hebrew calendar, King Artaxerxes' ascension year lasted two months. On December 17, 465 BC, the Egyptian New Year ended Artaxerxes' ascension year for the Egyptians. By the Egyptian calendar, King Artaxerxes' ascension year lasted four months.

Scientific Evidence

I have charted the length of King Artaxerxes' ascension year and listed New Year's Day for each of the three cultures below:

Hebrew (2 months)	Oct 17, 465 BC (Tishri 1)
Egyptian (4 months)	Dec 17, 465 BC (Thoth 1)
Babylonian (8 months)	Apr 14, 464 BC (Nisanu 1)

So New Year's Day was pivotal to how each culture numbered King Artaxerxes' years as ruler of Persia.

How the Years of King Artaxerxes' Reign Were Counted

Each of the three cultures counted King Artaxerxes' first year beginning with New Year's Day. For instance, the Hebrew culture started counting King Artaxerxes' first year on October 17, 465 BC. The Egyptians did not begin counting King Artaxerxes' first year until December 17, 465 BC. So each culture kept track of King Artaxerxes' years based on his ascension to power in August, 465 BC, then numbered the years on each subsequent New Year's Day. The following graph shows when each culture began counting King Artaxerxes' first official year.

Oct 17 465 BC	Year One Hebrew	
2 Month	Dec 17 465 BC	Year One Egypt
6 Month		Apr 14 464 BC	Year One Babylon

Since each culture maintained a distinct calendar, there were three ways to count King Artaxerxes' years. For example, on November 1, 465 BC, in the chart above, the Hebrews would have been in Artaxerxes' first year. But, the Egyptians and Babylonians were still in Artaxerxes' ascension year. On December 20, 465 BC, the Hebrew and Egyptian counting would have been in Artaxerxes' first year, while the Babylonians were still in the ascension year.

The Reign of Artaxerxes

Egyptian Papyri

Is it possible to prove that King Artaxerxes ascended to power in August, 465 BC?

I will use astronomy to show how Egyptian papyri from the 5th century BC Jewish Colony verify King Artaxerxes' ascent to power in August, 465 BC. In the following papyrus, the Hebrew date matches an Egyptian date in the 6th year of King Artaxerxes.

Kislev 21 = Mesore 1, Year 6 of Artaxerxes[43]

Kislev is the 9th Hebrew month. The Jewish New Year had occurred two months earlier on Tishri 1, meaning the Hebrews had incremented to King Artaxerxes' 6th year. However, the Egyptians were still in King Artaxerxes' 5th year since Mesore is the 12th Egyptian month. The Egyptian New Year was 35 days in the future from the dated text above.[a]

How do we find out the exact date the above papyrus was written? According to Chart B and scholarly references, the Egyptian date of Mesore 1 occurred on November 11. On November 11, the Hebrew lunar date was Kislev 21. Since the first day of a lunar month happens around a new moon, we know that a new moon occurred 21 days before November 11.

The correct lunar alignment must match King Artaxerxes' 6th year as referenced in the above papyrus. Since Artaxerxes became king in August, 465 BC, let's consider lunar data from the years 461, 460 and 459 BC, as taken from astronomical charts.

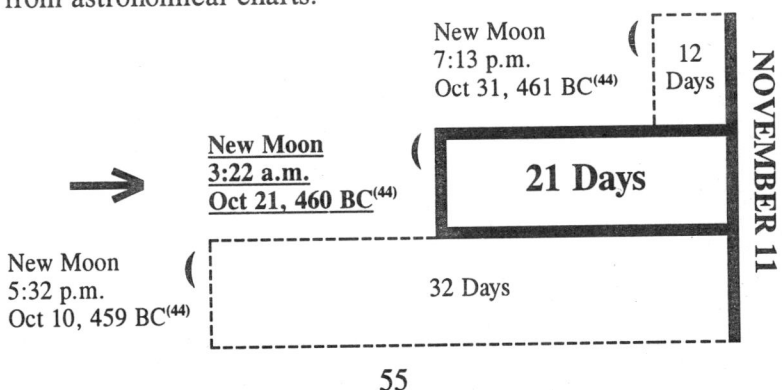

New Moon
7:13 p.m.
Oct 31, 461 BC[44] — 12 Days — NOVEMBER 11

→ **New Moon
3:22 a.m.
Oct 21, 460 BC**[44] — 21 Days

New Moon
5:32 p.m.
Oct 10, 459 BC[44] — 32 Days

Scientific Evidence

In the chart above, a new moon occurred 21 days before November 11, only in 460 BC. The lunar alignment of 21 days confirms King Artaxerxes' 6th year for the Hebrew culture. Moreover, this dated text confirms that King Artaxerxes ascended to the Persian throne in August, 465 BC.[b](45)

The following chart positions November 11, 460 BC, in the 6th Hebrew year; and the 5th Egyptian year for Artaxerxes.

Aug 24 460 BC	Year Six	November 11	Hebrew	
	Year Five (Egypt)		Year Five	Dec 16 460 BC / Year Six (Egypt)

So this papyrus supports the evidence found on the Babylonian Astronomical Text, showing that Artaxerxes' father was murdered in August, 465 BC.(36)(37)

Papyri from the Jewish colony at Elephantine, Egypt allow us to pinpoint specific dates for King Artaxerxes' reign. I have assembled the following chart based on actual double dated papyri from Elephantine, Egypt. All the papyri support the Hebrew counting for King Artaxerxes.

King Artaxerxes' Years (Hebrew Calendar)

Year Number	Start Date	End Date
Ascension	Aug. 465 BC	Oct. 16, 465 BC
1	Oct. 17, 465 BC	Oct. 6, 464 BC
6	Aug. 24 460 BC	Sep. 459 BC
14	Sep. 24, 452 BC	Oct. 12, 451 BC
16	Oct 2, 450 BC	Sep. 21, 449 BC
20	Sep. 18, 446 BC	Sep. 7, 445 BC

These papyri pinpoint King Artaxerxes reign. The results show that Nehemiah received the decree to rebuild Jerusalem on March 14, 445 BC.

Academic Support for Artaxerxes' Reign

Recent scholarship agrees that King Artaxerxes ascended to the throne in August, 465 BC. The following scholarly works support the conclusion of this study.

- Cambridge History of Judaism
- A Political History of the Achaemenid Empire

END NOTES:

[a] See Charts A and B in the back. Mesore is the 12th Egyptian month with the Egyptian New Year on Thoth 1. The Jewish New Year occurred on Tishri 1, the 7th Hebrew month. Kislev is the 9th Hebrew month. Since the dated text reads Kislev 21, the Jewish New Year occurred 2 months and 21 days before November 11, 460 BC, between August 23-25.

Some may believe that August 23-25 would be too early for the Jewish New Year in 460 BC. However, the late August date aligns with the modern Hebrew calendar. In the modern Hebrew calendar, every 19 years (235 lunar cycles) are about equal to 19 solar years. The lunar orbit is 2 hours, 4 minutes, and 24 seconds longer for every 19 year cycle. Carrying the calculation back to the 5th century BC, a period of 2,500 years, adds up to a difference of 11½ days. In the 20th century, September 5 is the earliest date possible for the Jewish New Year. Therefore, August 23-25, 460 BC is in perfect alignment.

The August 23-25 date for Tishri 1 means that Nisan 1 occurred as early as February 28, 460 BC. So the Passover could have occurred as early as March 14 in the 5th century BC. The papyrus discussed in this appendix sets ideal limits for calculating the date of the crucifixion in the 1st century AD.

[b] Should you want to do research. Study the article by S.H. Horn & L.H. Wood, "The Fifth Century Jewish Calendar at Elephantine," published by the Journal of Near Eastern Studies in January, 1954. The authors propound that King Artaxerxes ascended to power about December, 465 BC. The authors use two papyrus to support their assumptions. Aramaic Papyrus No. 6, reads "Kislev 18 = Thoth [17], year 21, the beginning of the reign of Artaxerxes I."[45] The date of Thoth 17 shows the document was written after the Egyptian New Year. Since this document designates Thoth 17 as the ascension year of Artaxerxes I, then King Artaxerxes would have ascended to the throne after Thoth 1. If Artaxerxes ascended to the throne after Thoth 1, then the first year of Artaxerxes would have began a full year later. However, all the double dated papyri do not support the authors' assumptions.

What were the authors' assumptions?

The authors rejected the Babylonian Astronomical Text that dates Xerxes' murder in August, 465 BC. The papyrus I have analyzed in Appendix A directly opposes the authors' assumption.

Next, the authors assume that a text equating the final year of a king to the ascension year of a new king can actually date when a power transition occurred. However, the evidence tends to show that Scribes could equate the final year of a king to the ascension year of the next king throughout the ascension year. The ascension year is a time of transition.

Finally, the authors believe that most of the papyri support their position. The authors' assumptions are so great that they throw out several well preserved papyri by blaming the dating on Scribal errors. The authors' work is highly suspect when actual information is annulled by the assumptions listed herein.

Appendix B

Day of Preparation

All the gospels indicate that Jesus died on the "day of preparation". What is the day of preparation?

Biblical law did not allow for any work on the Sabbath. Since preparing meals was considered to be work, people prepared extra food on Friday, the day of preparation for the Sabbath.

For example, when Israel wandered in the desert for 40 years, extra manna fell from heaven on Friday, the day of preparation for the Sabbath. People picked up enough manna to last until Sunday.

However, there is another way to explain the day of preparation in the gospel accounts. Biblical law did not allow for work on Nisan 15, the Feast of Unleavened Bread, which is a special Sabbath that could happen on a weekday.[a] In the case of a special Sabbath, the day of preparation could occur on any day of the week.[b]

If Nisan 15 occurred on a Thursday, then the Passover lamb must be slaughtered on Wednesday, Nisan 14. Following is a model for a Thursday crucifixion on Nisan 15.

Nisan 14 Wednesday	Nisan 15 Thursday
Passover Killed **Day of Preparation for the Passover** Exod. 12:6-7: Lev. 23:5	1st day of Unleavened Bread **Sabbath Rest** Lev. 23:6-8

In this example, the disciples would have killed the Passover on Wednesday. The last supper would have been eaten about 7:00 p.m., Wednesday evening. Jesus' arrest, trial and death would have occurred the following day, Thursday.

However, Matthew, Mark, and Luke write about two distinct days of preparation. The first is the "day of preparation for the Passover" at which the disciples prepared food for the last supper. So the disciples slaughtered a lamb on Nisan 14, making preparations for the Sabbath rest on Nisan 15.

> *The disciples left, went into the city and found things just as Jesus had told them. So **THEY PREPARED THE PASSOVER** [Killed the lamb] (Mark 14:16).* [c]

The second "day of preparation" mentioned by Matthew, Mark, and Luke occurred the day Jesus died. Since the first day of preparation was for the Passover, the second day of preparation was for the Sabbath[d]. Therefore, Jesus died on a Friday.[46] I have mapped the week of Jesus' death as follows:

Thursday Nisan 14	Friday Nisan 15	Saturday Nisan 16	Sunday Nisan 17
Last Supper	Crucifixion	Sabbath	Resurrection
Day of Preparation for the Passover	Day of Preparation for the Sabbath		

The primary reason for the confusion as to which day of the week Jesus died comes from the gospel of John. John portrays Jesus' death on Nisan 14. Yet, John also mentions two distinct "days of preparation". John mentions the "day of preparation for the Passover" in John 19:14, which is Nisan 14. John also writes of the "day of preparation for the Sabbath" in John 19:31, meaning Friday. So John writes of the two distinct days of preparation as the same day, which is Friday.

END NOTES:

[a] Lev. 23:6-8
[b] See John 19:14: The day is cited as the "day of preparation for the Passover" [NASB], which was Nisan 14.
[c] See Matt. 26:17-20 & Luke 22:7-14
[d] See Mark 15:42 & Luke 23:53-56

Appendix C
Lunar Dating the Crucifixion

Chapter 5 derived three "time-oriented" models from the Bible and astronomy to pinpoint the day Jesus died. Let's summarize the three models by stating the crucifixion occurred:

a) On Friday
b) In the years AD 31, 32 or 33
c) One to three days before a full moon

Models a) and c) above are critical to fixing the exact date of the crucifixion with astronomical data. Both models require that we find a lunar alignment with the full moon occurring on a Saturday, Sunday or Monday.

Since Daniel's time line points to AD 32, I will begin by depicting AD 32 as follows:

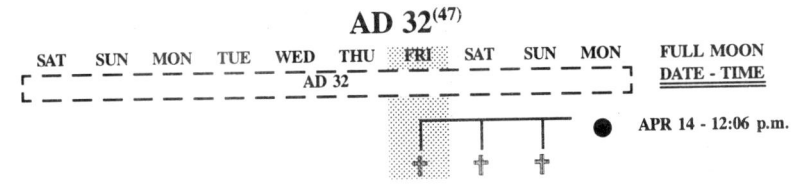

AD 32[47]

SAT	SUN	MON	TUE	WED	THU	FRI	SAT	SUN	MON	FULL MOON DATE - TIME
						✝	✝	✝	●	APR 14 - 12:06 p.m.

Viewing the graph above, we see a darkened circle on the right side in the Monday column depicting the full moon. The full moon occurred on Monday, April 14, at 12:06 p.m., which is shown in the far right column. Crosses appear before the full moon by 24 hours, 48 hours and 72 hours.

Friday's column has a cross. Months and years with a cross in the Friday column are viable choices for the crucifixion. Of course, months and years without a cross in the Friday column are eliminated as crucifixion candidates. I have shaded the Friday column to enhance the Friday requirement.

The year AD 32 meets all the conditions above. Jesus died on a Friday in either AD 31, 32, or 33. The full moon occurred on Monday, three days after the crucifixion.

Scientific Evidence

Lunar Data

Passover, in the first century, almost always occurred from March 15 to April 21.[a] However, considering all possible options, I will analyze lunar cycles from March 1 through May 1. The following tables present lunar cycles for the years AD 29 through 34.

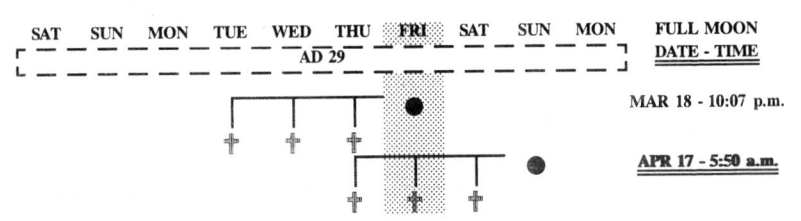

AD 29[48]

SAT	SUN	MON	TUE	WED	THU	FRI	SAT	SUN	MON	FULL MOON DATE - TIME

MAR 18 - 10:07 p.m.

APR 17 - 5:50 a.m.

Viewing the graph for AD 29, a cross appears in the Friday column showing one possible date for the crucifixion on April 15. In this case, the full moon occurred on Sunday, April 17, two days after Friday. Yet, AD 29 is not a good choice for the year of the crucifixion based on the historic setting in the gospels of Luke and John (AD 31 to 33).

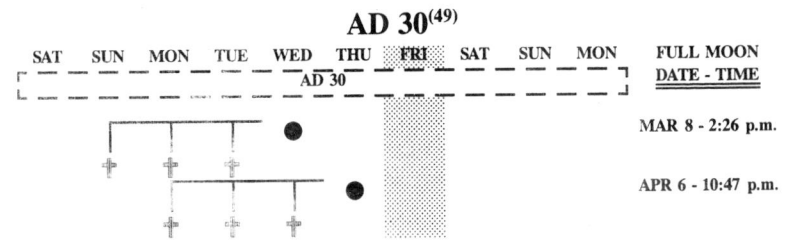

AD 30[49]

SAT	SUN	MON	TUE	WED	THU	FRI	SAT	SUN	MON	FULL MOON DATE - TIME

MAR 8 - 2:26 p.m.

APR 6 - 10:47 p.m.

Since there are no crosses in the Friday column above, AD 30 is not a viable year for the crucifixion.

Roman Catholics generally select April 7, AD 30, as the date of the crucifixion based on the scholarly assumption that Jesus died on a Friday with a full moon. Yet, AD 30 does not match any of the criteria. Jesus had to die on a Friday with a full moon occurring on either Saturday, Sunday, or Monday. Moreover, AD 30 does not match the historic setting found in Luke and John for the years AD 31, 32, or 33.

Lunar Dating the Crucifixion

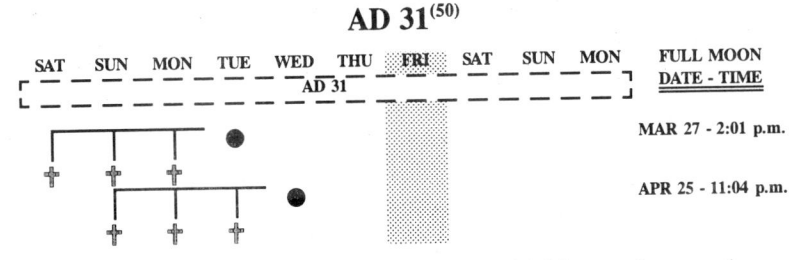

AD 31[50]

SAT	SUN	MON	TUE	WED	THU	FRI	SAT	SUN	MON	FULL MOON DATE - TIME

MAR 27 - 2:01 p.m.

APR 25 - 11:04 p.m.

Since there are no crosses in the Friday column above, AD 31 is not a viable year for the crucifixion. The year AD 31 does fit the historic setting found in Luke and John (AD 31, 32, or 33). However, AD 31 does not match a Friday crucifixion date with a full moon on Saturday, Sunday, or Monday.

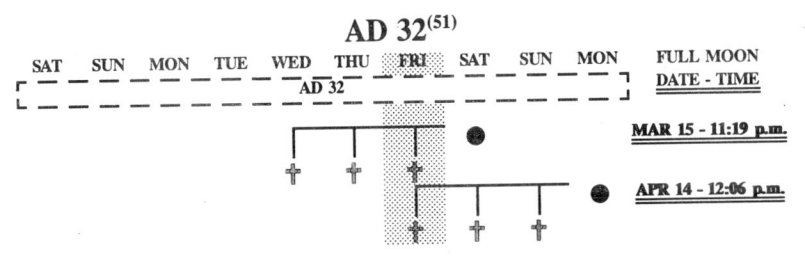

AD 32[51]

SAT	SUN	MON	TUE	WED	THU	FRI	SAT	SUN	MON	FULL MOON DATE - TIME

MAR 15 - 11:19 p.m.

APR 14 - 12:06 p.m.

Two lunar dates for the crucifixion emerge for the year AD 32. A full moon occurred on Saturday, March 15. The crucifixion would have been too early in the springtime on Friday, March 14. The second choice of April 11 meets all the criteria.

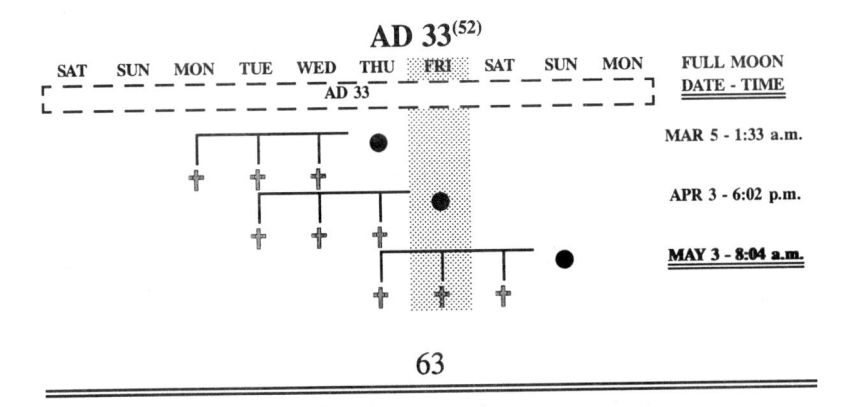

AD 33[52]

SAT	SUN	MON	TUE	WED	THU	FRI	SAT	SUN	MON	FULL MOON DATE - TIME

MAR 5 - 1:33 a.m.

APR 3 - 6:02 p.m.

MAY 3 - 8:04 a.m.

Scientific Evidence

Viewing the graph for AD 33, the only possible choice, though not a good one, is for May 1. The full moon occurred on Sunday, May 3. May 1 is a poor choice because it is very late in the spring.

Many theologians and church historians have picked the April 3 date because a full moon occurred on Friday. Early April is the perfect setting for the Passover. Yet, there is no cross in the Friday column with a full moon alignment on Saturday, Sunday, or Monday.[b]

Astronomy shows that a lunar eclipse occurred on Friday, April 3. However, a lunar eclipse offers no viable scenario for the crucifixion on April 3 since the sun had to be darkened, not the moon.

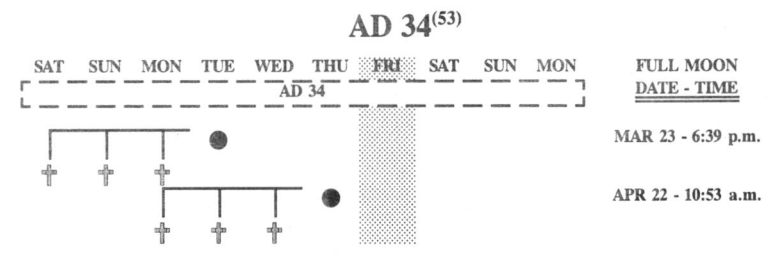

AD 34[(53)]

SAT	SUN	MON	TUE	WED	THU	FRI	SAT	SUN	MON	FULL MOON DATE - TIME

MAR 23 - 6:39 p.m.

APR 22 - 10:53 a.m.

Again, since there are no crosses in the Friday column above, AD 34 is not a viable year for the crucifixion.

Summary of Lunar Data

Astronomical analysis shows there are four possible lunar dates for the crucifixion. Two of these dates, March 14, AD 32 and May 1, AD 33, fall outside the March 15 to April 21 limits for the Passover in the first century. Eliminating these two dates leaves only two possible lunar dates for the crucifixion as follows:

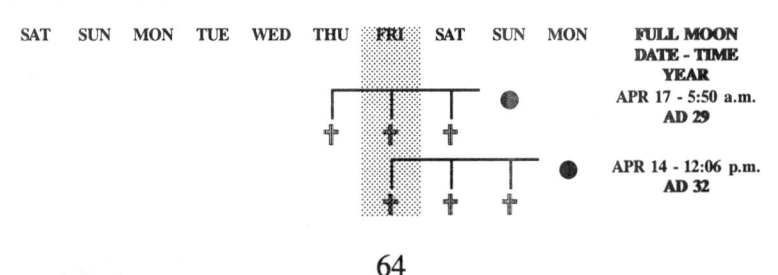

SAT	SUN	MON	TUE	WED	THU	FRI	SAT	SUN	MON	FULL MOON DATE - TIME YEAR

APR 17 - 5:50 a.m.
AD 29

APR 14 - 12:06 p.m.
AD 32

Lunar Dating the Crucifixion

The first candidate in AD 29 does not fit the historic setting found in Luke and John (AD 31, 32, or 33). Only the AD 32 date survives. Astronomy supports Daniel's prophecy with impressive accuracy, showing divine revelation.

END NOTES:

[a] Analysis of lunar cycles yields ideal times between March 18 and April 18 in the first century. However, the calendar could be off by up to three days relative to the moon. Therefore, the limits have been extended by three days to yield March 15 to April 21.

Read endnote [a] in Appendix A (page 57), where 5th century BC papyri support these limits, showing the earliest evidence for the Passover to be March 14 in the 5th century BC.

[b] Harold W. Hoehner, Professor at Dallas Theological Seminary, believes that Jesus died on Friday, April 3, AD 33.[54] Mr. Hoehner theorizes that the 173,880 days in Daniel's time line began on March 4 or 5, 444 BC, the 20th year of King Artaxerxes, and end on March 30, AD 33.

My research contradicts Mr. Hoehner's beliefs. Chapter 3 and Appendix A logically and clearly rebut 444 BC as King Artaxerxes' 20th year.

Mr. Hoehner accepts the biblical principle for counting a partial day as a whole day,[46] but fails to apply the biblical method to counting the 173,880 days. Moreover, Mr. Hoehner incorrectly adds the 173,880 days to March 5, 444 BC, to attain March 30, AD 33. I have taken the liberty to add 173,880 days to March 5, 444 BC, arriving at March 28, AD 33, a discrepancy of two days as follows:

Biblical count =	1 Day
476 years x 360 =	173,740 Days
Leap days =	116 Days
March 5 to March 28 =	23 Days
	173,880 Days

March 28, AD 33, happened on Saturday and must be Nisan 10. Placing Nisan 10 on a Saturday would not fit the biblical story of Jesus entering Jerusalem with crowds proclaiming him as the Messiah.

How could Mr. Hoehner solve this problem? Some may reason that Nehemiah's decree happened on March 7, 444 BC, instead of March 5, 444 BC. However, the new moon occurred at 10:30 PM on March 2, 444 BC, making the latest possible date for Nisan 1 to be March 5. Scholars have analyzed the papyri to show that at most the calendar was off by three days. I, too, have analyzed the ancient papyri wherein the first day of a Hebrew month always occurred from ½ day before the new moon to within 48 hours after the new moon. Only one papyrus possibly supports that the first of the month happened on the 3rd day after the new moon.

In my research, I have divided the 173,880 days found in Daniel by the time of one lunar cycle to show that Jesus could not have died on a Friday with a full moon. The evidence I have assembled in *Scientific Evidence for the Second Coming of Christ* fits flawlessly together with astronomical support. Daniel's time line points to Jesus' crucifixion on Friday, April 11, AD 32. The result of the AD 32 crucifixion date evolves 14,000 days from Jesus' entry into Jerusalem to the destruction of the temple. Could it be that we are witnessing God's rationale appeal to the world of Christ's imminent return and the relevance of two parallel generations of 14,000 days length?

Appendix D

Other Views of Daniel's Prophecy

Scholars interpret Daniel's "time-oriented" vision many different ways. These interpretations differ in the way they view the beginning and ending of Daniel's time line. Let's review the different interpretations by looking at the various dates possible for issuing of the decree to rebuild Jerusalem.

Decree to Rebuild Jerusalem

Scholars conclude that only three Persian kings could have issued the order to rebuild Jerusalem. Some believe Cyrus issued the decree between 539 and 536 BC. Others think Darius issued the decree in 520-519 BC, which confirmed Cyrus' original decree to rebuild the temple. Still others hold that Artaxerxes issued the decree to Ezra in 458 BC. Finally, many espouse Artaxerxes' decree to Nehemiah on March 14, 445 BC.

Following is a chart showing each Persian king, the date of each decree, and the specific purpose of each decree according to Scripture.

Persian King	Decree Date	Decree to Rebuild	Biblical References
Cyrus	539-36 BC	Temple	2 Chron. 36:21-23 Ezra 1:1-4; 6:1-5
Darius	520-19 BC	Temple	Ezra 6:6-12
Artaxerxes to Ezra	Mar 8, 458 BC	None	Ezra 7:11-26
Artaxerxes to Nehemiah	Mar 14, 445 BC	**Jerusalem**	Neh. 2:1-6

According to the biblical references above, Artaxerxes' decree given to Nehemiah is the only decree that specifically relates to rebuilding Jerusalem. All the other decrees were related to temple matters.

Scientific Evidence

Nevertheless, I can evaluate each date given in the chart above as to whether it is the actual decree to rebuild Jerusalem. According to Daniel's time line, 483 years must pass from the issuing of the decree to rebuild Jerusalem to the coming of the Messiah in AD 28. Jesus began his ministry in the 15th year of Tiberias Caesar according to Luke 3:1, which fell between August 19, AD 28 and August 18, AD 29.

So if you believe that Cyrus issued the decree to rebuild Jerusalem in 539 BC, then Daniel's time line must attain the 15th year of Tiberias Caesar in AD 28. This linear idea can be explained by the following graph.

Begin (X Year BC)   + 483 years   End 28 AD

On the left side of the graph above, insert any date believed to be the decree to rebuild Jerusalem. Next, add 483 years to find out if the time line attains AD 28, the year Jesus started his ministry. Consider how each decree from the chart on the previous page satisfies these criteria.

Persian King	Decree Date	Prophecy End Add 483 Years	Prophecy End Add 173,880 Days
Cyrus	539-36 BC	53 BC	60 BC
Darius	520-19 BC	36 BC	43 BC
Artaxerxes to Ezra	Mar 8, 458 BC	AD 26	March 31, AD 19
Artaxerxes to Nehemiah	Mar 14, 445 BC	AD 39	April 6, AD 32

Cyrus' decree in 539-536 BC attains 53 BC. Tiberias Caesar's 15th year occurred 80 years later. If 173,880 days are added to Cyrus' decree, the time line reaches 60 BC. So Cyrus' decree does not appear to be a good choice for the decree to rebuild Jerusalem.

The decree given by Darius to rebuild the temple in 520-519 BC only attains to 36 BC. Daniel's time line does not fit Darius' era.

Other Views of Daniel's Prophecy

Artaxerxes' decree to Ezra attains AD 26, two years short of Tiberias' 15th year. If 173,880 days are added to the March 8, 458 BC date, the time line arrives at March 31, AD 19. So Ezra's journey to Jerusalem in 458 BC does not appear to be a good choice for the decree to rebuild Jerusalem.

Obviously, only Artaxerxes' decree to Nehemiah yields the correct fit. Yet, some do not like this choice since it requires a 360-day year. I will discuss the 360-day year shortly.

The End of Daniel's Prophecy

In the above charts, I have taken a literal view of Daniel's linear prophecy in which the final seven years (the 70th week - Dan. 9:27) is yet to be fulfilled. However, some scholars believe that the entire prophecy was completely fulfilled at Jerusalem's destruction in AD 70. Those believing Daniel's prophecy is complete need a pair of scissors to cut and paste Daniel's words to fit their interpretation. In the following verses, I have moved the 27th verse to match this scholarly viewpoint.

> [26a]*After the sixty-two 'sevens,' the Anointed One will be cut off and will have nothing.* [27]***He will confirm a covenant with many for one 'seven,' but in the middle of that 'seven' he will put an end to sacrifice and offering. And one who causes desolation will place abominations on a wing of the temple until the end that is decreed is poured out on him.*** [26b]*The people of the ruler who will come will destroy the city and the sanctuary. The end will come like a flood: War will continue until the end, and desolations have been decreed.* (Dan. 9:26-27 distorted with scissors).

In this structure, the sequence of events usually places Jesus' 3½ year ministry as the first half of Daniel's 70th week, and Rome's destruction of Jerusalem and the temple in AD 70 as the end of the prophecy.

Scientific Evidence

The 360-Day Year

In the books of Genesis and Revelation, the length of a year is defined as 360-days. The 360-day year decodes Daniel's linear prophecy. From the decree to rebuild Jerusalem on March 14, 445 BC, I have added 173,880 days based on the 360-day year to attain April 6, AD 32, the day Jesus rode into Jerusalem with crowds proclaiming him as the Messiah. Exactly 14,000 days later, Rome set fire to the temple. The 360-day year uncovers the 14,000 days in Daniel's linear prophecy. In turn, the 14,000 days apply perfectly to the 21st century.

I have used Scripture to interpret Scripture. The 360-day year gives us a flawless interpretation of Daniel's linear prophecy. Are there other biblical prophecies that depend on the 360-day year?

Daniel received more "time-oriented" visions as detailed in the following chart.

Mysterious Number	**Reference**
2,300 Evenings and Mornings	Dan. 8:14
1,290 Days	Dan. 12:11
1,335 Days	Dan. 12:12
1,260 Days	Dan. 9:27
2,520 Days	Dan. 9:27

My research, based on the 360-day year, gives the explanation of these mysterious numbers and their flawless fit to the 21st century.

What do these mysterious numbers mean? Why are they in the Bible?

I invite you to read the fascinating details about these numbers in ***Mysterious Numbers of the Sealed Revelation***. This challenging book can be ordered from the "Preparations" section at the back of the book.

CHART A

Hebrew Calendar and Months

Hebrew Month	Corresponding Month	Number of Days	Sequence of Month
Nisan	Mar-Apr	30 days	1st
Iyar	Apr-May	29 days	2nd
Sivan	May-June	30 days	3rd
Tammuz	Jun-Jul	29 days	4th
Av	Jul-Aug	30 days	5th
Elul	Aug-Sept	29 days	6th
Tishri	Sept-Oct	30 days	7th
Marhesvan	Oct-Nov	variable*	8th
Kislev	Nov-Dec	variable*	9th
Tebet	Dec-Jan	29 days	10th
Shevat	Jan-Feb	30 days	11th
Adar	Feb-Mar	29 days	12th
We-Adar▲	Feb-Mar	30 days	13th

The Hebrew calendar cycles every 19 years. The intercalation of seven additional months in 19 years yields 235 lunar months which are nearly equivalent to 19 solar years. The intercalary month of We-Adar is inserted in the 3rd, 6th, 8th, 11th, 14th, 17th and 19th years of the lunar cycle.

* Marhesvan and Kislev, the variable months, contain either 29 or 30 days depending on the type of year. The variable month with 30 days is called "full" and those containing 29 days are called "defective." In a "complete" year, there are 355 or 385 days and both Marheshvan and Kislev are full. During a "normal" year, there are 354 or 384 days with Marhesvan having 30 days and Kislev having 29 days. Whereas in a "defective" year, there are 353 or 383 days and both Marheshvan and Kislev are "defective".

▲ We-Adar (2nd Adar, intercalary month)

CHART B

Fifth Century BC Egyptian Calendar

The Egyptian calendar consisted of 12 months, each containing 30 days. An extra five days were added after the 12th month to equal a year of 365 days. There were no leap years. Hence, New Year's Day, Thoth 1, moved one day backward every four years relative to the Julian calendar.

Month	Days	1st Day of Month 500 BC*	New Year's Day (Thoth 1)	Subtract x Days*
Thoth	30	Dec 26	500 to 498 Dec 26	0
Phaophi	30	Jan 25	497 to 494 Dec 25	1
Athyr	30	Feb 24	493 to 490 Dec 24	2
Choiak	30	Mar 26	489 to 486 Dec 23	3
Tybi	30	Apr 25	485 to 482 Dec 22	4
Mechir	30	May 25	481 to 478 Dec 21	5
Phamenoth	30	**Jun 24**	477 to 474 Dec 20	6
Pharmuthi	30	Jul 24	473 to 470 Dec 19	7
Pachons	30	Aug 23	469 to 466 Dec 18	8
Payni	30	Sep 22	465 to 462 Dec 17	9
Epiphi	30	Oct 22	461 to 458 Dec 16	10
Mesore	30	Nov 21	457 to 454 Dec 15	11
Epagomenai	5	Dec 21	453 to 450 Dec 14	**12**

449 to 446 Dec 13	13
445 to 442 Dec 12	14
441 to 438 Dec 11	15
437 to 434 Dec 10	16
433 to 430 Dec 9	17
429 to 426 Dec 8	18
425 to 422 Dec 7	19
421 to 418 Dec 6	20
417 to 414 Dec 5	21
413 to 410 Dec 4	22
409 to 406 Dec 3	23
405 to 402 Dec 2	24

* How to Use This Chart

You can calculate a Julian date for any Egyptian month in the 5th century BC, using this Chart. For example, Chapter 3 says that Phamenoth 25, 451 BC is July 6. How do we find out the date was July 6? First, column 3 shows Phamenoth 1 in 500 BC occurred on June 24. Second, columns 5 and 6 tell us to subtract 12 days for 451 BC

June 24 - 12 Days = June 12

Third, since the date is Phamenoth 25, we must add 25 days to June 12.

June 12 + 25 Days = July 6

References

1. Flavius Josephus, *The Complete Works of Josephus*, translated by William Whiston, (Grand Rapids: Kregel Publications, 1960), "Wars of the Jews," bk 6, ch 4, s 5, p 580.
2. Ibid., p 580.
3. Herman H. Goldstine, *New and Full Moons, 1001 BC to AD 1651*, © 1973 by The American Philosophical Society, Independence Square, Philadelphia, p 90.
4. Sir Robert Anderson, *The Coming Prince*, Kregel Publications, Grand Rapids, Michigan 49501, © 1984, pp 119-129.
5. M.A. Dandamaev, *A Political History of the Achaemenid Empire*, Translated by W.J. Vogelsang, Published by E.J. BRILL, New York, © 1989.
6. Thiele, Edwin R., *The Mysterious Numbers of the Hebrew Kings*, Zondervan Publishing House, Grand Rapids Michigan 49506, © 1983, p 71.
7. Ibid., p 71 & 229.
8. Ptolemy, (Claudius Ptolemaeus), *The Almagest*, Translated by R. Catesby Taliaferro, *"Great Books of the Western World"*, Vol 16. Ptolemy, Copernicus, Kepler. Edited by John Maynard Hutchins and Mortimer J. Alder. University of Chicago, © 1952 by Encyclopedia Britannica, Inc., p 172.
9. Herman H. Goldstine, *New and Full Moons, 1001 BC to AD 1651*, © 1973 by The American Philosophical Society, Independence Square, Philadelphia, p 40.
10. Ptolemy, (Claudius Ptolemaeus), *The Almagest*, Translated by R. Catesby Taliaferro, *"Great Books of the Western World"*, Vol 16. Ptolemy, Copernicus, Kepler. Edited by John Maynard Hutchins and Mortimer J. Alder. University of Chicago, © 1952 by Encyclopedia Britannica, Inc., p 137.
11. Herman H. Goldstine, *New and Full Moons, 1001 BC to AD 1651*, © 1973 by The American Philosophical Society, Independence Square, Philadelphia, p 42.
12. Ibid., p 43.
13. Thiele, Edwin R., *The Mysterious Numbers of the Hebrew Kings*, Zondervan Publishing House, Grand Rapids Michigan 49506, © 1983, p 71 & 229.
14. Ptolemy, (Claudius Ptolemaeus), *The Almagest*, Translated by R. Catesby Taliaferro, *"Great Books of the Western World"*, Vol 16. Ptolemy, Copernicus, Kepler. Edited by John Maynard Hutchins and Mortimer J. Alder. University of Chicago, © 1952 by Encyclopedia Britannica, Inc., p 136.
15. Emil G. Kraeling, *The Brooklyn Museum Aramaic Papyri: New Documents of the Fifth Century BC from the Jewish Colony at Elephantine*, Published for the Brooklyn Museum by the Yale University Press, New Haven, © 1953 by Yale University Press, pp 132-133.
16. Herman H. Goldstine, *New and Full Moons, 1001 BC to AD 1651*, © 1973 by The American Philosophical Society, Independence Square, Philadelphia, p 46.
17. Ibid., p 131.
18. S. H. Horn & L. H. Wood, "The Fifth-Century Jewish Calendar at Elephantine," *Journal of Near Eastern Studies* (January 1954), p 11.
19. John Zachary, *Threshold of Eternity*, Harvard House, P.O. Box 24221, Denver, CO 80224, © 1989, p 182, note b.
20. S. H. Horn & L. H. Wood, "The Fifth-Century Jewish Calendar at Elephantine," *Journal of Near Eastern Studies* (January 1954), pp 11-12.
21. Herman H. Goldstine, *New and Full Moons, 1001 BC to AD 1651*, © 1973 by The American Philosophical Society, Independence Square, Philadelphia, p 47.
22. Harold W. Hoehner, *Bibliotheca Sacra*, "Chronological Aspects of the Life of Christ," October 1974, pp 332-348.
23. Michael Kalafian, *The Prophecy of the Seventy Weeks of the Book of Daniel*, University Press of America, New York, © 1991, pp 3-6.

24 Harold W. Hoehner, *Bibliotheca Sacra*, "Chronological Aspects of the Life of Christ," October 1974, pp 348.

25 J. K. Fotheringham, *The Journal of Theological Studies*, "The Evidence of Astronomy and Technical Chronology," April, 1934, pp 146-62.

26 Robert C. Cowen, *The Christian Science Monitor*, "British Scientists find an Astronomical Clue to help date Crucifixion of Jesus," January 3, 1984, Vol. 75, pp 27, 30.

27 Herman H. Goldstine, *New and Full Moons, 1001 BC to AD 1651*, © 1973 by The American Philosophical Society, Independence Square, Philadelphia, p 87.

28 E. J. Bickerman, Chronology of the Ancient World, Cornell University Press, Ithaca, New York, © 1968, pp 25-26.

29 "Calendar, Hebrew," Encyclopedia Judaica, Keter Publishing House Jerusalem Ltd., © 1972 Keter Press Enterprise, Jerusalem, Israel, Vol 5, p 49: **(Year length varied 352-56 Days)**.

30 Herman H. Goldstine, *New and Full Moons, 1001 BC to AD 1651*, © 1973 by The American Philosophical Society, Independence Square, Philadelphia, p 87.

31 John Zachary, Threshold of Eternity, Harvard House, P.O. Box 24221, Denver, CO 80224, © 1989, p 183, note e).

32 Ibid., pp 15-23.

33 Ibid., pp 18-19.

34 Ibid., pp 9-14.

35 Dolan, David, *Israel: The Struggle to Survive*, Hodder and Stoughton, London, © 1991 by David Dolan, pp 171-172, 219.

36 Sachs, A.J., Pinches, T.G., & Strassmaier, J.N., *Late Babylonian Astronomical and Related Texts*, Brown University Press, Providence, R.I., © 1955.

37 Dandamaev, M.A., *A Political History of the Achaemenid Empire*, E.J. Brill, Leiden, The Netherlands, © 1989, p. 234.

38 Parker, Richard A. & Dubberstein, Waldo H., *Babylonian Chronology: 626 BC - AD 75*, Brown University Press, Providence, R.I., © 1956, p. 17.

39 Thiele, Edwin R., *The Mysterious Numbers of the Hebrew Kings*, Zondervan Publishing House, Grand Rapids Michigan 49506, © 1983, p 53, 180.

40 E. J. Bickerman, *Chronology of the Ancient World*, Cornell University Press, Ithaca, New York, © 1968, p 117.

41 Herman H. Goldstine, *New and Full Moons, 1001 BC to AD 1651*, © 1973 by The American Philosophical Society, Independence Square, Philadelphia, p 45.

42 S. H. Horn & L. H. Wood, "The Fifth-Century Jewish Calendar at Elephantine," *Journal of Near Eastern Studies* 13 (January 1954): p 8.

43 Horn, S.H. & Wood, L.H., The Fifth Century Jewish Calendar at Elephantine, *Journal of Near Eastern Studies* 13 (January 1954): pp 9-10.

44 Herman H. Goldstine, *New and Full Moons, 1001 BC to AD 1651*, © 1973 by The American Philosophical Society, Independence Square, Philadelphia, p 45.

45 Horn, S.H. & Wood, L.H., The Fifth Century Jewish Calendar at Elephantine, *Journal of Near Eastern Studies* 13 (January 1954): pp 9-10.

46 Harold W. Hoehner, *Bibliotheca Sacra*, "Chronological Aspects of the Life of Christ," July 1974, pp 241-264.

47 Herman H. Goldstine, *New and Full Moons, 1001 BC to AD 1651*, © 1973 by The American Philosophical Society, Independence Square, Philadelphia, p 87.

48 Ibid., pp 86.

49 Ibid., pp 86.

50 Ibid., pp 86.

51 Ibid., pp 87.

52 Ibid., pp 87.

53 Ibid., pp 87.

54 Harold W. Hoehner, *Bibliotheca Sacra*, "Chronological Aspects of the Life of Christ," January 1974, pp 47-65.

PREPARATIONS

Does the Almighty direct people? My research using scientific dating of prophetic events shows that you and I are being directed. You must make the choice to seek truth about God.

Ask and it will be given to you; seek and you will find; knock and the door will be opened to you (Matt. 7:7).

Perhaps you want to know more about Christianity. You can receive FREE literature from the section below by ordering any of the booklets that interest you. Write to us for FREE literature, or call the prayer line for prayer. People at the prayer line are not there to answer questions about *Scientific Evidence for the Second Coming of Christ*. Yet, Christians are waiting to pray with you. If you have a question about *Scientific Evidence for the Second Coming of Christ*, write to Harvard House.

For Prayer Call: (303) 433-0033

Check off ✓ your interests or the whole package. A suggested donation of $.50 each will help in covering the costs of ministry.

- ☐ Did Christ Really Rise From the Dead?
- ☐ Why Did Christ Have to Die?
- ☐ Who is This Man Who Says He's God?
- ☐ Religion or Christ: What's the Difference?
- ☐ What's the Appeal of the New Age Movement?
- ☐ How Do You Live the Christian Life?
- ☐ Knowing God Through the Whole Bible
- ☐ The Way Back: Returning to Christ
- ☐ Have I Been Too Bad to be Forgiven?
- ☐ Why Does it Make Sense to Believe in Christ?
- ☐ 10 Reason to Believe in a God Who Allows Suffering
- ☐ Why in the World am I here?
- ☐ What is a Personal Relationship With God?
- ☐ Praying with Confidence

Concerned For Your Friends?

Do you believe others should know about the message in *Scientific Evidence for the Second Coming of Christ.* Enlist in the spiritual battle with prayer and by purchasing a comfortable number of copies for people to read. Interested in world evangelism? Order *The Cutting Edge*.

HARVARD HOUSE LITERATURE

☐ ***Threshold of Eternity*** $9.99
☐   Number of Copies _____ x $9.99 x Discount Below $_____
    (i.e. 5 copies = 5 x $9.99 x 0.75 = $37.45)

☐ ***Mysterious Numbers of the Sealed Revelation*** $2.99
    (Available After September - 1994: You can Preorder)
☐   Number of Copies _____ x $2.99 x Discount Below $_____
    (i.e. 5 copies = 5 x $2.99 x 0.80 = $11.95)

☐ ***Scientific Evidence for the Second Coming of Christ*** $2.99
☐   Number of Copies _____ x $2.99 x Discount Below $_____
    (i.e. 10 copies = 10 x $2.99 x 0.75 = $22.40)

DISCOUNT SAVINGS

Scientific Evidence/Mysterious Numbers		Threshold of Eternity	
2 Copies (Times 0.85)	$5.00	2 Copies (Times 0.80)	$15.95
5 Copies (Times 0.80)	$11.95	5 Copies (Times 0.75)	$37.45
10 Copies (Times 0.75)	$22.40	10 Copies (Times 0.70)	$69.90
20 Copies (Times 0.70)	$41.85		
50 Copies (Times 0.65)	$97.15		

☐ ***The Cutting Edge*** $7.00
    Monthly Newsletter(Postage/Handling for 1 Year)
    (For people interested in keeping contact & evangelism)

    Add for Shipping & Handling
    (excluding monthly newsletter)   Minimum $1.75
    If ordering over $20.00, add 5%
    to the total order for Shipping/Handling   _____
    Colorado Residents Add 3.5% Tax   _____

                TOTAL _____

HARVARD HOUSE

P.O. Box 24221

Denver, Colorado 80224-0221

Call Toll Free for Orders

1-800-906-5500

VISA/MC